A PASTOR'S \
THROUGH B

MW00614391

THE
BEAUTIFUL
UGLY
TRUTH

GWEN BRAGUE

TWO PENNY
PUBLISHING

Two Penny Publishing
850 E. Lime Street #266
Tarpon Springs, Florida 34688
TwoPennyPublishing.com
info@TwoPennyPublishing.com

For permission requests and ordering information, email the publisher at: info@twopennypublishing.com

Library of Congress Control Number: 2021915374

Paperback: 978-1-950995-47-9
eBook also available

FIRST EDITION

For information about this author, to book event appearance, or media interview, please contact the author representative at: info@twopennypublishing.com

Praises For

THE BEAUTIFUL UGLY TRUTH

I have known Gwen for almost 30 years and have always admired her genuine passion for ministry. She has been steadfast and faithful to pursue and trust God at every turn of her life. So it is no surprise that she would open her heart and life to help other couples even through the raw details and expressions of her personal journey and pain. Her story gives hope that through faith and trust in Christ, we can overcome any obstacle and truly LIVE again! Thank you, Gwen, for sharing your innermost thoughts and experiences in order to facilitate the reconciliation of hearts to God and to marriage. You are a treasure to behold!

Candace Ramsey

Co-Lead Pastor at Restoration Church in Atlanta, GA

Who are you going to call when your marriage has been attacked by betrayal? Therapists, friends, and family can be supportive and comforting. They may even have some answers. However, when you need a true miracle, you call on your heavenly father who knew you even before he formed you in your mother's womb. Gwen's story provides hope and purpose for damaged marriages through sharing her experience of God's power to heal when you trust in his word. If you are feeling devastated and alone, I recommend that you read this book and hear God's word for your life.

Shannon Barnes, PhD
Licensed Professional Counselor
Family and Marriage Counselor

Some stories you read. Others you see lived out. This story is one I've seen lived out over decades. I've watched Gwen and Mark walk through the hard days—the "we need a new start days"—and I see them now. This book is raw, honest, and most of all, it's authentic. But most importantly, it's about seeing what God does when we reconnect with Him, and with our spouse.

Tim Walker
Co-author of *Sex180* (Baker Books)

Gwen Brague's story *The Beautiful Ugly Truth* is real, raw, and incredibly brave. Gwen pours her heart out onto the pages as she dives head-first into rarely explored places within marriage, relationships, and couples navigating ministry together. Gwen and Mark's journey, from their lowest places to their greatest triumphs as a couple, will inspire many to examine the legacy their own relationships are leaving for future generations.

Stephen and Ali Tessitore

Business Leaders and Social Media Influencers

What I love about our friendship with The Bragues is what you see is what you get: a realness, a vulnerability and love of Jesus that is tangible. *The Beautiful Ugly Truth* is just that. Yes, Gwen shares the bitterness of betrayal, but then she shares the sweetness of redemption. Gwen's pursuit of Jesus through the pain is inspiring and encouraging for anyone who has gone through crushing life change or for anyone who needs a reminder that Jesus is King. Mercy and grace are the heroes of this story because it's His Story. He's the redeemer. He's the restorer. He's the reconciler. He's the Truth.

David and Leanna Stein

Campus Pastor at Revolution Church in Canton, GA

Marriage and ministry can be interesting partners. At times they seem almost like rivals pulling people in opposite directions. Knowing that God is at the heart of both lets us know that there is a way for these two institutions not only to "co-exist," but to thrive together. Gwen tells the painfully honest story of trying to get to that place. She shares the hurt and the disappointment that many like her have experienced. She also brings a message of hope and restoration. Betrayal is real. And it is devastating. But there is a way back. It's not easy and it's not quick. Still, it is available to those who are willing to do the hard work of recovery. Gwen and Mark are two who have walked that walk. They have a story to tell that needs to be heard. This is not an easy story to tell. It takes two people who are brave and strong. I commend their courage. Marriage and ministry are great partners when each is done the way God designed. I believe this story can both help those who have experienced similar struggles as well as prevent others from making the bad choices that lead to that desperate place.

Dr. Thomas Tanner

Lead Pastor at Riverstone Church, Kennesaw, GA

Having known Mark and Gwen for more than 30 years, I have always been touched by her authenticity and sincere passion for her Heavenly Father, her family, and helping people. This book is a game changing book because in it a respectable person gets gut level honest about life and marriage. We're all broken, all of us, and more than we are comfortable admitting. This book tells the story of a broken marriage that had no hope and very little chance of survival...and Father God did what he always does when His children do things His way. He resurrected this marriage; and even though it's still imperfect, it is flourishing and that gives us all hope! Gwen gets very real and personal about how a wife can hang in there, forgive, and trust again. I hope many people get the message found in this book! Its a message of hope that you can live again even after unimaginable hurt, betrayal, and pain. Not only can you live but you can live with joy, fruitfulness, and LIFE just like Mark and Gwen are now doing. I love this book and its author and the One Who makes all things new!

Chuck Ramsey

Lead Pastor at Restoration Church in Atlanta, GA

"All I knew was Christ had entered our storm." For anyone who ever needed to feel the peace and presence of God in the midst of heartache, this story captures the beauty that glimmers beneath our pain, with truths that will linger in the still places of your soul long after it is read.

Jennifer Walker RN BSN

Co-author of the *Moms on Call* book series.

Gwen Brague takes the reader through her personal journey of betrayal, displaying the beautiful details of God's grace woven within her pain. Her honest testimony as a pastor's wife and daughter of divorced parents, connects her reader to a brokenness many understand and have experienced.

Stephanie Broersma

Reclaimed Ministry

To the strongest men I know:
Mark, Elijah and Noah.
You guys have taught me to be brave and made me feel
loved and secure.

To the 63-68% of pastor's wives in pain
and whose husbands are suffering in silence....
you got this.

God is with you.

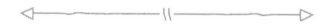

To inquire about having Gwen speak at your next event,
visit gwen@reconnectinglives.org

Contents

Introduction

Someday Everything Will
Make Perfect Sense.

During one of the most broken seasons in my life, when one plus one did not equal two, I saw this sign in a little hospital gift shop:

"Someday, everything will make perfect sense."

Even though I didn't purchase the sign, that statement proved to be a gift for me and brought me hope. I wasn't sure how God would make sense out of this particular heartbreaking season in our marriage, but I knew He could. I also believe someday, everything you are walking through will make perfect sense too.

Purpose is defined by, The reason for which something is done, created, or for which something exists. I knew there was a purpose for this season we walked through. It is for this reason, these words containing our story are on these pages.

There is something about the season changing from winter to spring that ignites and awakens my soul. The spring season delivers us from the harsh reality of the cold, dark winter days and nights. During winter, I often wonder if it'll ever get warm again. If the grass will ever return to green, and if my feet will ever see my flip flops. After surviving what seems like a 'death' winter season, spring enters and the sky becomes baby blue, the air feels clean, and the birds sing us a new song.

I remember a time when I felt I was experiencing the 'winter season' of my soul accompanied by the 'winter season' of our marriage. This was a time not too long ago. My soul was barren, and our marriage felt dark, dreary, and gloomy. Do you ever wonder if life, relationships, or marriages will make sense again? Some days are filled with complete joy and some days are just plain difficult. Some days laughter fills every void, and some days there is no laughter. When two people who pledged their lives together are broken, or when relationships between parents and children are constrained by a breakdown of communication, the distance between fulfillment and void hardly makes sense.

Mark and I had been married for seventeen years and had two teenage boys when we hit our 'winter season.' Elijah was thirteen, and Noah was eleven. We had been serving as full-time pastors for fifteen years when everything we believed in began to be tested: our marriage, our family, Mark's job as a pastor, where we lived, and our whole livelihood. As our house of cards began to crumble under the weight of deception, nothing made sense. There were days I wondered whose life I was living. It was a season when health issues, betrayal, and pornography surfaced. Pastor Mark and I lay in the wake of its destruction. I asked God questions amongst my rants of anger, "Could our marriage survive?"

"Would our lives return to normal?"

I judged Mark because it was the only thing that made sense to my broken heart. I wanted a reason for the pain I was experiencing. I wanted to point my finger at the pain and do my best to get rid of it. However, the center of my pain was tied to the person I loved most in my life. There were days I knew my flesh and my heart would fail, but God's Word reminded me that He was my strength. King David said it best,

> *"My flesh and my heart may fail, but God is the strength of my heart and my portion forever."*
> *Psalms 73:26 (ESV)*

I have learned now that trials make me confident, because they draw me to God and His Word. I discovered during my greatest need, He was with me and guiding my path. Often, we blame God for our misfortune, don't we? I remember wondering why He brought me to this season. During this time I was convinced He was asleep. However, God reminded me He was with me. He promised in His Word,

"I will never leave you nor forsake you."
Hebrews 13:5 (ESV)

Your trials may not make any sense to you currently, but someday, everything will make perfect sense. This is not my story in its entirety....just parts of it. The most difficult parts of my story are strangely the best parts. I share the hardest parts with you because God reconciled our marriage, healed my body, and made my heart whole in Him. Life can still be challenging, but we can partner with God and engage His presence for the journey. Perhaps the hardest parts of your life will become your best parts as well. Everyone's journey is special and unique to them. I was not sure how mine would turn out, but I was determined. I believed God for an abundant life as He promised in John 10:10, with or without the pastor.

I love my family, but we are not perfect. Far from

it. During the most challenging times, I discovered my identity was in God and not in who I married. I found emotional healing through counseling, but most importantly, God revived my wounded soul. God loved me without exception. God restored me like He promised and exposed lies embedded in my thinking.

Now, if there is anything I can do to help others love God and discover their voice in this world, I will risk my reputation for it. Listen as you read my story and see parts of my life unfold. Within it, you will find the evidence of a personal God. A God who speaks. A God who still speaks.

I'll have to take you through the pages of my journals in order to explain all the details of what it felt like: the searing fear and blinding hope. I recorded my thoughts and prayers there and poured my heart out onto the paper. It helped me remember all God had done in my life. Like Joshua, when he crossed over into the Promised Land, he told the leaders to gather stones because he wanted to remember what God had done (Joshua 4). My journals and part of their entries are at the top of each chapter as stones of remembrance of a faithful God. I am now laying the pages out there to be seen, held, and felt.

When God speaks, things happen. When God spoke in Genesis, He began creation. He separated light from darkness, land out of water, put the stars in the sky, and created all the animals and all of humanity. What was once dark, void, and without form, God spoke, and creation emerged. A formless world was never the same. He is still that amazing God who desires nothing more than a relationship with all of humanity. Maybe there are places in your life where you need God to speak as well. The hurt places, the lost places, the void places. I promise He can speak. And once He does, it can change the course of your life forever. Jesus did not only speak peace to the storm, but He spoke peace to my storm. He not only spoke life back into Lazarus, but He spoke life back into me and my heart.

As you take this journey with me, ask yourself, "Where do I need God to speak into my life?" This is a story of a woman, a wife, a mom, and a daughter who happens to be a pastor's wife. Sometimes God will stop at nothing to change you. I mean really change you. For me, it was my marriage to my husband, the pastor. This is my confession of a pastor's wife and my survival story of a season when betrayal and pornography had their grips on my marriage. Sadly, this story is not uncommon. Statistics show that more than half the pastors in a pulpit today secretly struggle with pornography. I share this story because pastors and their wives need a safe place to heal. Mark and I have made it to the other side of this devastating winter season and we are now alive again. It was not a quick fix. Our story will reveal that, but we can both say we are much better for it.

"Now to him who is able to do far more abundantly than we can ask or think according to the power at work in us"
Ephesians 3:20 (ESV)

It seems natural to start at the beginning. But the beauty of the story is in the ending of a horrendous season in our lives. The rest of our story is still being written on the pages of my journals. You will find that the most difficult seasons in your life will point to an extraordinary God that can reach far beyond what we ask or think (Ephesians 3:20). The cold, brittle, sometimes unbearable winter days will always give way to the renewing warmth of a beautiful spring season. If you are in the middle of winter, hang on. Spring is right around the corner.

I wrote this book for pastors and their families, specifically for couples who have experienced betrayal while serving in ministry areas of the church. I also believe *The Beautiful Ugly Truth* can help rebuild any marriage that has experienced the heartache of betrayal or the secret of pornography exposed.

As the wife of a pastor, I unintentionally put pastors on a pedestal. I believed they were the next closest thing to God. No doubt being a pastor is a unique calling, but pastors are humans.

So like flying a plane, it might be a turbulent ride through these pages. When darkness is upon us in areas we never expected, the truth will be your light that one day will lead you to health and wholeness. My hope is this book will be a flashlight for your journey.

If you are in need of hope in your relationships, in your marriage, or if you are in need of a God that still speaks, I encourage you to read on.

Dear Father,

Sometimes life doesn't make sense. We love you. We serve you. We think others love and want to serve you as well. But we live outside the garden now. The garden where Adam and Eve embodied a beautiful picture of marriage. However, sin reached that garden. Our world is broken now, and so are we. I know you have redeemed us and have overcome the world with your Son's life. So, we invite you into the most vulnerable places in our hearts; the garden of our souls. Where we need you to speak and reveal yourself. Change us by the power of your presence. Reveal our wounds, heal our heartaches. Cause us to be courageous in our journey to true inner healing. We bring all of us to all of you. May we find you there, Lord. We give you permission to make sense of our senselessness.

We love you. We trust you.

Amen

Ask yourself, "Where do I need God to speak into my life?"

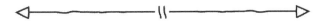

Sometimes our answers to prayers
may not look or feel like
God's answers, but *trusting*
Him with the process is the most
important thing we can do.

chapter one
The Betrayal Unfolds

*Every time we are "wronged,"
we go through temptation, anger,
and entitlement. You will be
led away into more temptation
when you choose not to forgive.*

Our marriage was broken. I was exhausted by our disconnection. I did not think I even had enough strength to fast. Yet, it was in the midst of a twenty-one-day Daniel fast when God began to speak to my heart about the coming excavation. Mark and I had been married for seventeen years. I often prayed for our marriage to be healed over the last five years. Though I could not put my finger on it, something just seemed off between us. Mark had been emotionally absent from our relationship for years. He wasn't mean to me, just emotionally unplugged. Every time I asked Mark if we were okay, he would say what I wanted to hear, and we would keep trudging along. I didn't feel as confident in our marriage as I once did which brought on feelings of anxiety. I believed these feelings were all about me and my personal struggles. I began to question a lot of things during this season.

Deep inside me, I knew we had built our relationship with Jesus as our firm foundation. I trusted when the storms of life came, that our family would remain. But this storm felt like hurricane-force winds. And though I trusted God, it did not take away from the intensity of the storm we were entering into. We lived in Florida at the time and knew what hurricane-force winds were like. There are preparations that need to happen upon weathering a storm. Little did I know God was directing me with such a preparation during this fast.

For me, praying and reading scripture was a part of my preparations. But counseling was going to be a huge part of weathering this storm. What I learned in counseling was the application applied to what I was reading in scripture. I had, for many years, remained physically fit. I had awakened to faith and believed scriptures for years. Scripture was my guiding light for walking in health. But I was unaware of all my emotional inner wounds and how they played a vast role in being healed completely.

It was January, and though it was a little chilly outside, I remember being near the front door and the sun shining through the sidelights. It was a warm place by our home office, and I pulled out my bible and asked God for His direction. Our family did a twenty-one-day Daniel fast at the beginning of each year, and this year was no different. I always prayed for our family, and in the last few years I had asked God specifically to wake up Mark. As I prayed over our marriage, I felt led to this particular scripture.

> *"For nothing is hidden except to be made manifest; nor is anything secret except to come to light. If anyone has ears to hear, let him hear."*
> *Mark 4:22-23 (ESV)*

This verse brought me momentary relief. God was hearing my heart's cry and leading me through scripture. However, I also had a strange sense that something was hidden. I didn't know what was hidden, but I was tired of the distance between Mark and me. I often second guessed my feelings during this season and often try to explain my feelings away.

The most recent feeling I had that something was hidden was with a relationship my husband had with another staff member at our church. He was serving as an associate pastor there. This woman had cried tears of joy upon Mark's arrival as a new staff member, and had opened up her hurting heart over her troubled marriage in multiple church gatherings.

I remember the first pang of discomfort I felt upon seeing her arms wrapped around my husband's waist at a church gathering. My husband met her before I did. He had been spending ten days at a time at the church before our family arrived three months later. This staff person was engaging, beautiful, funny, and had children the same age as ours. She seemed like any other staff member, except for her arms and their lingering presence around my husband's waist after a church event. Being a youth pastor's wife years prior, I would see kids hug my husband, maybe a lingering hug, but otherwise they had been harmless. However, to see a grown woman's arms, let alone another staff member's arms, wrapped around Mark's waist was unsettling to me. I was caught off guard and speechless. As shocked as I was, I didn't want to overreact in that moment.

Once we arrived home from the gathering, I remember telling Mark specifically how the event made me uncomfortable. He replied, "I was surprised by that too. I thought it was you standing behind me." His response was enough to set the event to rest. But as any woman would, my radar and 'spidey - senses' were up whenever she was around.

The red flags slowly began to get more frequent when

she announced her divorce some months later. From that point on, it was often that I would walk into the church and catch a glimpse of them hugging or Mark patting her face. It escalated into repeated hugs and kisses on the cheek, of course, while saying their goodbyes to one another with each meeting. And with every hug, with every pat, with every kiss on the cheek goodbye, we would get in the car and when it was safe to say, I would ask him to stop showing her such affection. I was shocked how it was flaunted right in front of me every Sunday only to be assured nothing was going on. I hated how their interactions made me feel. I didn't feel safe. I felt needy, weak, angry, and anxious.

However, every Sunday, he would reassure me they were just friends. Many months passed with relentless questions and reassurances after each interaction with one another. We would leave church, meetings, small groups, and our own house, and I would wonder if I was making this all up in my own head. Mark would tell me that I was just overreacting. I wanted to trust my husband, but his actions made me feel otherwise.

One Sunday, months later, we left the church, and I knew that I couldn't take it anymore. During an informative mission trip meeting right after service, I turned around to speak to Mark only to find him sitting in a chair getting his back and hair stroked by her. Did no one in this whole church not notice this? At that moment I was crushed, and I was done.

Every occasion we discussed their flirtation gestures, Mark assured me that there was nothing inappropriate going on. This time was different. I was done being polite. We got in the car and I held back my thoughts until I couldn't any longer. We drove to lunch that day and after the kids were out of the car, I asked, "If you are having an affair with her, would you at least have the courage to tell me?" My question to him this time was a little more colorful with explicit language. I couldn't believe I would even be asking my husband that question. He was a pastor and my life partner. We had safeguarded our relationship for years, but something was different this time. I was angry and hurt. Mark knew the years of my past hurt prior to our marriage. But he seemed blind to the inappropriate way his actions were playing out in his life. His blind spot in his soul was like a driver's blind spot in a car. Other passengers might see blind spots easily, but the driver does not. I didn't believe him that Sunday when he tried to reassure me once again. So, I began my relentless search for evidence. I began to search emails and text messages to no avail. I could not find one email and not one phone text message between those two. More questions and anxiety lingered in my mind.

Somewhere inside of me, I believed the "thing which

was hidden" would surface. Some days I felt up to the fight for my marriage, but other days I was scared and anxious. I believed the scales that covered Mark's eyes could be removed, and the truth could eventually set us free; it just didn't happen immediately or without damage.

I never felt validated in my repeated confrontations with Mark. Their interactions kept being played off as nothing for me to worry about. It was hard to distinguish which was causing me more hurt, Mark's affectionate gestures towards another staff member or the fact that this man, who shared my life, my heart, and my children would not validate my observations. I felt exposed without a protector, and the one who promised to protect and do life with me was distant. My anxiety and stress levels were at an all-time high.

I was desperate for relief from this ground that felt so faulty. I remember seeking professional help from a licensed mental health counselor because of my high anxiety levels during this season. The sad thing was I hadn't linked the anxiety I was feeling to our marriage issues. Feelings are so personal. We have feelings and thoughts and capture them as our own. Counseling was a true gift for me. Going to counseling was a huge set-up for when the "things that were hidden" would be exposed in our marriage. It made perfect sense looking back now. I remained in counseling and constantly hoped for a resolve for my anxiety. It is true what they say about counseling, that what might initially take you to counseling is usually not what you need counseling for.

Looking back, I watched this season play out like a movie and often wondered what movie set I had been dropped in on. This season did not seem real in my life. All I leaned on during this time was the passage in Mark 4:22 (NLT),

"For everything that is hidden will eventually be brought into the open, and every secret will be brought to light."

Just three days later, after I had outright asked him if he was having an affair, Mark did the unimaginable. With complete knowledge of how uncomfortable I was with their friendship, Mark once again cast my feelings aside. On Wednesday nights we would take our boys to youth group and drop them off at the church. Mark and I would usually go to dinner to desperately try to reconnect with one another. This particular Wednesday, after we dropped our guys off at youth, Mark opened the back seat of our car and invited her to our Wednesday night dinner date. I screamed a silent scream inside and fought hard to hold back the tears of my tender heart as she jumped into our backseat to join us for dinner. It was so hard for me to believe at the time God was using the event to expose more truth. I remember opening my own car door once we arrived at the restaurant to get out, only to watch Mark open her door. I sat at dinner feeling devastated and defeated. I honestly felt my voice meant nothing. I watched them talk to one another till I was sick to my stomach.

However, during that conversation she offered to update Mark's phone. And during dinner, the connection was revealed to me. I watched as she showed Mark how to update his phone. They could talk and text Blackberry to Blackberry and it didn't show up on his normal text message app. My first thought was, could this be how they have been communicating all this time? God was bringing to light that which had been hidden.

I took the opportunity the next week to hold my husband accountable by looking up his messages on his phone. I was driven by my hope in a future together. I was petrified to learn the truth but more unsettled not to know the truth. Before taking the leap of faith and looking, I chose to get away for the night. I had scheduled a training class the next morning at a pregnancy center to help mentor other young ladies. I went and spent the night at one of my friend's house. She knew Mark and me, and that things were not going well for some time now in our marriage. I shared my concerns with her and her husband. They were a safe place for me. They had seen the inconsistency with Mark's actions, and strangely, that gave me some comfort. I was conflicted and torn about whether or not to get away. I knew I needed it for my own sanity, but was fearful of leaving Mark alone even though he had the boys. This was one night my faith had to be bigger than my fears.

I shared every detail with my friends that evening. They prayed that God would not tarry much longer and that which was hidden would finally be revealed. They prayed specifically for Mark, for our marriage, and for the strength for me to endure. I remember towards the end of the prayer, Dean prayed this, "Come quickly, Lord. Come quickly into this situation."

Have you ever prayed or heard someone pray and felt God bend low to hear? Nothing had changed that evening with Mark and me regarding our situation, but I knew something shifted. I got dressed the next morning and walked to my car with a heavy yet determined heart to go to my one-day training event. I remember hugging my friends goodbye, getting in the car, and turning on the radio only to hear the Chris Tomlin version of "Amazing Grace."

My chains are gone,
I've been set free,
My God, My Savior has ransomed me
And like a flood His mercy reigns
Unending love, AMAZING GRACE!

Honestly, I felt the chains of our situation. The literal weight of them I had carried for months lifting off me that particular morning. I could not explain it. The heaviness in my heart, my mind, and my spirit lifted away when I began to sing that song. I turned the radio all the way up in the car, rolled down my windows, stuck my left arm out the window, and I sang to the top of my lungs. Somehow, I knew God was moving on our behalf that morning. My heaviness was being exchanged with a different garment, if only for a moment. It was the most freeing, exhilarating feeling I had felt in months.

Please know, **sometimes our answers to prayers may not look or feel like God's answers, but trusting Him with the process is the most important thing we can do.** At God's right timing, you will begin to sense God moving your mountain. He will enter your storm and will speak peace into it. For me, at that moment, I was willing to partner with Him and not my own emotions. All I knew was Christ had entered our storm. I still cannot explain it; I just knew something shifted within me.

The beauty of the storm is that He can speak peace to it. And when the storm gives way to the peace-speaker, the clouds lift, and the peace resides.

"Let us go to the other side."
Mark 4:35 (ESV)

It was only four days later when God began exposing all of the lies within our marriage. It was another Wednesday. I will never forget, February twenty-fourth. We call the day, D-Day. D stands for Discovery Day. I was getting ready for Bible study and getting the boys ready for school. I felt my first prompting to check Mark's phone. Mark was in the shower while I was drying my hair.

Because of the dinner we had exactly a week prior, I knew where to go on his cell phone to check his messages. My heart was racing as I left our room to walk into the kitchen. I grabbed his phone off the island and began my search. I felt the lump in my throat and almost started crying before I typed in his passcode. My hands were shaking, and my mind was racing. I was mixed with emotions. I wanted to find some kind of validation, but on the other hand, I didn't. Validations would only prove what my heart was trying to tell me all along.

Immediately, my heart was shattered by my discovery of their text thread from the day before. "Hi Honey, how are you doing today?" Mark asked her. She responded by telling him how badly her day had been going. He began to reassure her that her day would get better and said all the things he would say to me when I was having a bad day. He texted about how he was looking forward to seeing her at small group. They ended the thread with how much they missed each other and how they couldn't wait to be together. My heart sank. The same small group I had asked him to guard himself from, they were looking forward to. I experienced the strangest mix of emotions. I was not going crazy. All my woman's intuition was right, but to what expense?

Anger began to swell up in me like a wave up against the storm wall. What happened to my peace a few days ago? I wanted to go back and sing with my arm hanging out the window of my car. I want freedom. I knew God had spoken to the storm, but it would get worse before it got any better. If I had any hopes of survival, I needed to hold onto Christ's unshakable promises. At this point, I felt it was all I had left. The next emotion was sadness and a sickness deep down in my very being. It was like a release. All those red flags were for a reason.

Mark was still showering and the boys were getting ready to walk out the door to go to school and I was a mess. How could I process all this in one morning? I felt as if I had just been in a head-on collision; shocked. What should I do with this newfound information?

The very next thought I had was to get the kids ready for school and let Mark go to work. It sounded like a good thing to do. Looking back now, I know God's love was directing me. But in the moment I felt utterly lost and completely devastated. I wondered if this was how my mom felt the first time she realized my dad was having an affair? Was this what countless others feel like?

Grief. Numbness. Sucker punched. Anger. Sadness.

As everyone left the house, I tried desperately to get dressed for bible study. It was almost an impossible feat. This new knowledge left me shocked and dazed.

I remember Mark didn't kiss me goodbye that morning. I remember every detail about the day as if it had been seared into my mind. I went to my friend's house for the bible study with my mind on autopilot. As I was driving, the gravity of our situation was beginning to sink in and I contacted my friend, Ginger, who lived in Georgia. I needed my friend. She and her husband had walked through something similar. She gave me great counsel and listened to me vent. I didn't know how our situation would play out, but I knew that my friend's marriage had survived. On the way to bible study I also called my mentor, Carol (who was a licensed mental health counselor) and she suggested we meet with her and her husband at her office that evening if I could arrange it.

Lastly, before I arrived at bible study, I called Dr. Sandy, the counselor I had seen prior. I left a message at her office to please call me. My world felt like sand beneath my feet, movable and shifting. I was going through the motions with my body, but with my mind completely distracted and numb. I knew I was going to talk to Mark at some point that day, but had no idea what I was going to say. I even wondered if he would be mad that I looked at his phone.

After bible study, I lingered numbly so I could talk with my friend. I nicknamed her "my spiritual B12" friend. She was a friend God had placed in my life for this season. She was wise and did not put up with foolishness. She would call a spade a spade and to her, at this moment, the devil was a spade.

She had sensed my mood was not my jovial self during the study. She walked me to my car and asked me what was wrong. I told her that I thought my husband was having an affair. I told her about the text messages I had read earlier, and she offered some advice and prayed for me.

The advice was this, "The first thing you are going to do when you confront your man about this is.... put on your lipstick. Because anytime you are going in for the blow, you want to look good." That made me smile in the uncertain moment of my life. However, I took her quite seriously. I looked into my purse, grabbed my lipstick, and stared vacantly into my rearview mirror as I applied my lipstick.

I was minutes away from meeting Mark and all I had planned was to pray and freshly applied lipstick. My counselor called me back in those moments driving to meet Mark. I kept telling her I didn't know what to say or do. I must have said it several times on the phone, and the voice of reason in my counselor said, "Gwen, you do know what to do...think about it and let me ask you a question. Biblically speaking, what should you do? If you have gone to him several times to no avail, what should come next?"

I replied, "Take someone with you?"

And then she said, "And if that doesn't resolve it, then biblically, what do you do next?"

I answered sheepishly, "Go to the pastors and elders." Surely that was not the answer. I almost said it as a question.

But she replied, "That is correct. Sometimes you have to let others know."

The only lingering question for me was, how? How would I get the strength to confront him one more time? And if he denies it again, how would I tell the pastor and elders?

I remember arriving at the church offices nervous, but girded with the truth this time. I went to Mark's office and asked him if he had a minute to talk. I didn't have a script in mind and I wasn't sure how all of this would play out. The office was buzzing with all the staff members that afternoon. It was a Wednesday, and preparations were being made for evening meetings. I asked Mark if we could step outside. We walked outside the office, and I looked into those same green eyes that had once captivated me, and I confronted him.

"You know I love you, but I am not going down this path with you anymore," I said seriously and sternly. It was an intense moment but not argumentative. It was like God had complete control. I was sad, hurt, and beyond angry. With my voice cracking, I told him I had come to him on numerous occasions with no resolve regarding this matter. This time would be different. I told him I had read their text messages this morning and knew what he had said to her. I told him I was done and came to give him a choice.

He seemed stunned by all this information. Maybe he was shocked he had finally gotten caught. Or perhaps he had never heard me so resolute.

He was still in denial and maybe his disbelief, in part, was because he was hearing the real truth for the very first time. I did not give him a chance to try to deny or explain himself anymore. I once again told him I had found their text messages and I wasn't going to do this anymore. I told him if he stepped into a small group with her, the boys and I would leave him and go back to Georgia. Period. I let the sentence sink in for a minute before I said anything else. His other option was to come to counseling with me. I felt those words just needed to sit in the atmosphere for a minute. He looked puzzled and shocked, but I saw tears in his eyes. Maybe the tears were for the love he had for the boys. I was unsure of a lot of things. Sadly, I didn't feel like the tears could possibly be for us, because of his actions.

He was in charge of all of the small groups at the church, and his small group was one of many. It would be no small task for him to miss his very first small group of the quarter. But I had backbone this time. I told him again if he did not come to counseling with me tonight I would assume he chose her and I would go back to Georgia with the kids. It was his choice.

The first words he spoke to me was to ask me if there was any other way. His question made me more hurt and mad. It was not the first time he had pushed my feelings aside. I immediately thought of the conversation I had just had with Dr. Sandy earlier. I told him we could go tell the senior pastor right now. I was trying to deal with a very inappropriate situation quietly, but I didn't see any other way. He actually agreed, and we headed to the senior pastor's office. I was not sure how this conversation was going to go. Mark was not saying much to me on the walk back into the office. I knew our situation was getting ready to interrupt the Wednesday afternoon preparations.

We knocked on the senior pastor's office door and asked if he had a minute. He invited us in but immediately knew something was not quite right. I began to tell him all about the last few months. After telling the pastor all of the details, I was shocked by his response. The first words out of the pastor's mouth were actually to defend Mark and his actions. Not only Mark's actions, but the actions of the other staff members too. I felt like my head was going to explode. I had a difficult time believing what I was hearing. How was this possible? It did not take long before I began to feel myself grow more and more angry. The pastor continued with his response by telling me Mark was a nice guy and maybe the last several months were misunderstandings on my part. All the inappropriate gestures, the small group meetings, no telling how many text messages they exchanged, and all of this was Mark's attempt to be friendly to another female staff member. I had experienced the red flags, the boyfriend gestures, and who knows, all the meetings they had been alone in for months. My feelings had been denied repeatedly by Mark's responses, but no one was going to belittle my assessment this time, not even the senior pastor. I was through with the lies and the overlooking of his actions.

I remember telling the senior pastor that if he was going to defend my husband's inappropriate actions, along with other staff members' actions, then I was getting up and 'getting the hell out of here.' At first I could not believe I said that, but I did. My grief in the moment had given way to anger. I was not going to be the quiet little pastor's wife anymore. The pastor looked at Mark and said, "I think she is serious. You have my permission to cancel your small group this evening and go see this counselor if you want to, Mark." I left the office without Mark as he gathered some things from his office, but it would not be long before Mark was at the house.

After the meeting with the pastor, I was not happy. I was hurt. This time it was by the shepherd of the church. It seemed like the most important thing to the pastor was keeping his staff together and not our marriage.

Moving forward from that meeting, there seemed to be a great amount of grace from the pastor towards Mark. However, something seemed unsettling there. Mark was released during the daily work hours for counseling appointments, but future meetings with the pastor didn't seem right. I could not put my finger on it for months. Sadly, Mark's denial would not be the only denial uncovered during this season. Denial is not a respecter of persons or spiritual position.

That night our mentors and friends, Carol and Dean, met with us. Carol knew Mark as a previous staff member. She knew his character and his integrity, and the type of person he was. This behavior was not indicative of his character, which is why I prayed so long for him to wake up.

Carol started asking Mark questions. One of which was "When did her feelings become more important than Gwen's feelings?" His initial response was, "They haven't." And she replied, "It does not seem like the math is adding up, Mark. Gwen has asked repeatedly for you to stop showing affection towards this person, and you have not." Carol again repeated the same sentence once more. She began telling stories of Mark as a young youth pastor. She reminded him of who he was; as a person, a friend, a pastor, and a husband. She spoke of the man he was and the character he always displayed as a former staff member. She went on to remind him of the boundaries he had always set. There was no finger-pointing. Carol was just reminding Mark of who he was and pulling back the layers of deception. Dr. Sandy could not have said those things to Mark because she did not know Mark before. For God to have chosen Carol and Dean to speak to Mark the first night was pivotal. I was thankful, grateful, and angry all at the same time. Carol said the man she knew was not the one who would hold another woman's feelings over his wife's well being. Once again, he tried to define his actions.

Carol persisted, trying to help Mark see how he had put this woman's feelings far above my feelings. I saw my strong, God-loving, six-foot-tall husband begin to break.

I believe God was breaking through to him, and in the moment, something began to happen. He was quiet. I watched him process what Carol was saying. He began to cry as he and Carol kept talking. Could she be cracking the code? As he cried, I heard him begin to talk to me quietly. "I am so sorry. I am so sorry. Did I do this to us? I am so sorry." He just kept saying that he was sorry and he never meant to hurt us. Finally, that which was hidden was showing glimmers of light. It was as if I was seeing him for the first time in years. To this day, he describes that moment as the first real day of clarity in years.

I cannot say my response to his apology was tender, loving, or gracious that night. I was relieved the truth had come to light, but it felt like a double-edged sword. There was no great joy in this revelation. My feelings were finally validated and crushed, knowing my husband was having an inappropriate relationship with someone else. My only satisfaction was found in my prayers being finally answered to some degree. But fear felt like a constant companion as we walked through many dark days, months, and years ahead.

I looked into Mark's eyes and said words I did not know lived inside of me. It's amazing how hard I fought to get us to this moment, only to feel a rush of anger. I thought I would be happy to be here or maybe a little satisfied he was finally aware of what he had put us through. But I felt nothing but pain, anger, and great sadness. I apologized to Carol for saying nasty things back to Mark in her office, but she graciously told me she had heard worse and we continued. She kept talking to Mark to make sure he was aware of the gravity of our situation. He began to say all the right things I had longed to hear. It had been years since I saw into his soul through his eyes. My trust in him was damaged. The journey back would take some time. I remember him asking me if seventeen years of marriage meant nothing to me. I had no answer of assurance that evening.

Mark now says, trust is lost in "buckets" and only gained back in "drops." One drop at a time. If you are here, drops are like seeds. It just takes time to develop.

Carol was a critical player in the initial confrontation. God led her to us. After hours of emotional upheaval, I cannot even remember if Mark and I spoke in the car on the way to pick up the boys at the youth group function. So much had happened in our friend's office. Moving forward I began to wonder how I would act normal in front of our boys.

There were still bridges to be crossed and counseling to be done. I had just finished with my twenty-one-day Daniel fast, which I believed sustained me during this upheaval. After the initial meeting with Carol, we began seeing Dr. Sandy weekly. I would go one week, and Mark would go the next. Then we would both go to counseling the following week. After Mark's admission of lines being crossed, we began the work to see if our relationship could withstand this storm. Dr. Sandy encouraged Mark this was the time to get any other secrets out. As scary as it sounded, our foundation would remain faulty without truth in all areas of our relationship. I wanted to believe him, but I was convinced there was more to be discovered. We were weeks past the exposure of the affair and weeks into counseling when one night before I went to bed, I felt God's whisper in my heart saying, "Eat and drink this week, be ready. There is still more to this journey."

I sensed more fasting would need to take place. I remember asking Mark if there were more secrets, but he assured me he had told me everything. However, during the weeks that followed, I found out that we were just scraping the top of what lay hidden and beneath the surface. This season was like the skin of an onion, many layers deep. There were such hard, hard days ahead of us.

"For in the time of trouble He shall hide me in His pavilion; In the secret places of His tabernacle He shall hide me; He shall set me high upon a rock...
I would have lost heart unless I had believed that I would see the goodness of the Lord in the land of the living."
Psalms 27:5&13 (NKJV)

I was often reliving some of my hurt by the unresolved emotional wounds in my own early years with my parents' divorce. Their story felt like paying compounded interest to our story. On the most difficult days I had to remind myself this season was strangely an answer to my prayers. I had asked God for the last five years to heal my marriage. I wanted and asked for the truth over and over. I just didn't realize how painful the unfolding truth would be.

I also recognized early on, partnering with unforgiveness and anger would not be beneficial to me or our journey. It's not to say I did not feel those emotions. I surely did. I was so hurt and so angry. I asked many questions in my own head often. How could Mark bring us here? What happened to him? When did he let his guard down?

The storm was still present, I just had to trust God to get us to the other side. I knew my healing had to involve forgiveness but my flesh was so, so weak.

Your story may be different than ours but one thing is for sure, God is present. **I know the storm can distract you from His presence but He is there.** I remember often having the feeling of, "I can't take this anymore," and God would remind me His Son took my place. His Son, Jesus Christ, paid the price of sin; our sin, my sin, his sin, her sin, whoever's sin, and nailed it to the cross and traded His righteousness for it. I promise, it's the best trade. Trust

Him if you are in the middle of trouble. The days you don't have the strength to keep going, find a quiet place and lean into His presence. He is there for you. He was there for us. Yes, there was more to our story, typically there always is. There were days I felt I could not see clearly but God's peace was my guiding force. So whatever trouble you are involved in, take courage and steadfast your heart, friend. God is with you! Victory is at hand. Trust Him as you go to the other side.

Dear Jesus,

This is a lot. Even as I type this, my heart senses the storms others may be walking through. Memories flood our mind and we seek your peace. You are so acquainted with the storms in our lives. They do not frighten You. Your peace resides within the storm. You spoke and the winds and the waves obeyed Your voice. I pray for peace over life's storm, now. I am so thankful you are in the process. I pray you will be ever present in someone else's process. I pray our senses will come alive to your presence. Pain knows no bounds BUT neither do YOU. We live in a fallen world. Lord, I pray if we are blaming You for our situations and our storms, by saying things like, "If only you would have been there," we would pause. Help us realize You are the One who will deliver us through.

Our safety is with You. Peace, Peace. Shalom Peace. Break the authority established by chaos. Our hope is in You.

In Jesus Name, Amen

If you find yourself in this particular storm and need someone to reach out to, contact us at www.reconnectinglives.org.

We have a prayer wall there and the emails come directly to us. Reach out, we will respond.

Or write your prayer on the following page.

_____

_____

_____

_____

_____

_____

_____

_____

_____

_____

_____

_____

_____

_____

_____

_____

_____

_____

_____

_____

_____

_____

◁————————— || —————————▷

chapter two
My Beginnings

It is amazing how the pain in our past wants to find itself in our future.

The first time I felt the pull of the Lord on my heart was in a little country church in Tennessee. It smelled of stale perfume, and I remember the hard wooden pews. In front of me were little old ladies with too many bobby pins and big fat curls to count. Often at the pulpit was my uncle John, the fire and brimstone pastor. And beside me sat my brother and my mother. On this particular evening service, the invitation to give our heart and life to Christ was placed before the congregation. I left the church crying because I hadn't walked to meet my uncle and Jesus at the wooden altar. My tender heart was clearly disturbed all the way home at having missed my great moment. I thought I was going to be condemned to hell now. I was only six-years-old.

Yes, the story could have just ended there, but my mom

knew better. She asked questions on the way home as to why I was so quiet. When I was able to tell her all that was on my heart, she only encouraged me. She said when we returned home, we could go inside to pray. We knelt beside her bed with our knees planted on the hardwood floors. I still remember her black and white tapestry bedspread lying across her 1960s style solid wood-carved bed. The black fringes gave me something to hang on to as my mom led me in a prayer to receive Jesus as my Savior. We were a sight to behold as we cried and held each other tightly. My spiritual journey started right there in my mother's arms, in our little three-bedroom house in East Tennessee, just a few miles from a church with the powerful, life-changing presence of God. A seed was planted in the soil of my little six-year-old heart. The sinless life I expected to follow did not exactly materialize. But I felt the first tug, and it was the first in a long line of encounters with God. I remember my father not being at that service even though he still lived at home with us at the time.

For the next several years, I went to church and always tried to do the right thing. Now, I know God was with me and protected me in ways I was not aware of. I think about how He spared my life in the midst of many decisions I made on my own. There were painful moments to come in my life, however, Christ had captured my heart at a young age to usher me through some difficult seasons.

One of those difficult times in my young life would come just a few years later, while I was nine and my brother was twelve. The sun was shining, and the yard was calling our names as it did on many afternoons. Inside my house, a heavy feeling lingered like deep wintery snow. It was the day my mom and dad announced their divorce. Shattered and scared, I did what I was told and navigated the strange new way of life the best I could. It's no wonder I struggled for years regarding my identity. Fathers provide a sense of identity for their children. Though he lived in the same town, our family relationship changed. I became fearful.

I loved my father, but it was difficult for a nine to understand the inner workings of a marriage and its demise. Slowly and quietly, a distrust began to tear its way into my heart. The fear that entered was not invited, but would follow me for years. Fear waited to pounce any time my heart sought to trust someone. Many relationships were fractured moving forward from that day. Often my thoughts told me not to give my whole heart to anyone in fear that they would leave too.

The fear I experienced so early in life was not the only lasting emotion stemming from my parents' divorce. I was at a critical time in the development of who I was as a person. I wanted someone to protect my heart and give me an identity. Our home was broken, so I felt broken.

Because the loss felt so great and I didn't understand how to process the pain, I began to develop a tough girl exterior. I didn't understand that my name and identity had been established in the heavens long before I breathed my first breath. But I thought if there was a God, why would he let bad things happen. I longed to feel normal like all of my other friends who had a daddy at home. I wanted to be my daddy's princess, but decided early on a princess was too dainty for my heart to behold. On Tuesdays and Saturdays, my dad would pick me up for his visitations. He told me he loved me those days, but my tough girl persona was already being formed from the pain of his daily absence. History tells a story, our story.

Philosopher George Santanya said it best, "Those who cannot learn from the past are doomed to repeat it."

From nine to twenty-four, I tried my best to navigate my own life. However, it takes a long time to drive without a clear direction. During those years, it felt like I was on a road trip without a GPS. I followed the lead of my own desires. Don't get me wrong, I eventually got to where I was going, so I thought, but life seemed to take quite a few extra turns, and I still felt lost.

By the age of twenty-four, life was not cutting it for me. I had made many mistakes along the way and tried to cover them up with youthful pride. I was in and out of relationships that never satisfied my heart. Painful events and memories left me longing for something more. Often, I felt I wasn't good enough for others, just like I thought I wasn't good enough for my dad to stay home. Thankfully, I was at the end of my rope and sought freedom from this way of thinking. I needed something different. I wanted to start over, but the last place I remembered feeling peace was at that little church in East Tennessee.

I lived in Georgia at the time, waiting on tables at a nearby restaurant. A weekly five-hour trip to go to church seemed out of the question. So, I did the next best thing. I asked a friend at work if he knew of a church nearby. My friend told me of the church he grew up in, but he was cautious to show up there years later. His life was an emotional wreck like mine. But I was convincing, and we went the next Sunday. I remember that Sunday weeping before God, asking Him to take over my life and the mess I created. I am certain, looking back, God was with me. I felt anew even though my circumstances were still the same. God would take over my life from that point on, but it still wasn't immediately sunshine and lollipops. The journey to restoration would take some time, and with it many more tears. My emotions felt underdeveloped, and often, I would do my best to suppress them and keep moving on. When I finally opened the door to my heart and let God lead the way through my life, I became more self-aware of my wrecked past. As I became a student of scripture, He would begin to speak and change me forever. His unconditional love rescued my heart just like He promised He would. But we would have years of work to heal it fully.

I still had to deal with my distrust of men and my aching need to know who I really was. God knew what my heart needed. And to know who I was in Him meant I had to let down some of the sturdy walls surrounding my heart. It also meant I had to practice forgiving those who let me down so I could begin to trust again. I had to know what trust felt like to discover who I was in God. I believe there are different ways God chooses to heal us. Sometimes it's miraculous, but oftentimes, it's about the journey.

As a child, we physically grow and change on the outside, but our emotions are also forming within us. I learned it was important as we are growing older not to let our emotions get trapped or shut down when we experience pain. At this point in my life, I had many trapped emotions from my past. This was my first step in the healing process, allowing God to heal those early hurts. I was bleeding and broken emotionally on the inside, and it shaped my thoughts and reactions on the outside. I desired deeply to love and be fully loved. Little did I know the path of pain and looking back in order to move forward was actually the pathway to healing. **Pain leads us to healing.**

God taught me if something was physically broken, you don't cut off what is broken just because there is pain associated with it. I learned as long as God was the Great Physician, there was hope for my pain on the inside. However, when we feel emotional pain, our temptation is to cut off those feelings. We build inner walls around our hearts and we don't like to forgive. We hold onto offenses, and we start making inner-covenants with ourselves. A covenant is an agreement; a lease, deed or legal contract. An inner covenant is something we make with ourselves in order to protect our heart.

Usually, an inner covenant will have words like *never* or *ever* or *always*. For example, "No one will ever hurt me like this again," or "I will never be poor."

I would never minimize someone else's pain. I can only speak from my experience and the many opportunities I have experienced by cutting off my emotions. It will only cause you more anguish in all areas of your life and in your relationships. It will stunt your growth and hurt you and others more in the long run.

Two questions to ponder:

- What was one of the most important lessons I always carry with me?
- How do you begin to heal your emotions when you are hurting and in pain?

Forgiveness. This is where many of us get tripped up. We want someone to pay for our pain. We want to be justified, but we are afraid that if we forgive, we are letting the other person off the hook. Forgiveness is not for the offender, but rather for you. Forgiving those who hurt you releases you from the past offense. The word "offense" has its root meaning in the word "bait." When we don't forgive and choose to hold onto the offense, we are on the hook— like bait. Forgiving is not about "letting the offender off the hook;" **true forgiveness is about letting yourself off the hook.**

I am still learning to forgive. It's not a "one-time fix-all" event. Forgiveness is a process. It's about surrendering our right to get even or be right. Forgiveness is about handing our offenses over to God, and letting Him deal with the justice side of it. **Forgiveness is "for-giving" our hurts, betrayals, abandonment, and all our wounds over to the One who can heal us.** Our inward struggle comes down to trusting in God to right the wrong against us. It's about partnering with God and being released from our past. The freedom God brings when we release the wrongdoings is supernatural. I have had many opportunities in my life to forgive. I have even asked for others to forgive me. Remember none of us are perfect.

Forgiveness is about walking in freedom, and it's about your freedom. **Forgiveness is your pathway to freedom.**

Christ paid the ultimate debt. He purchased my freedom and yours so we can be who Christ has called us to be. He has called us to be loved, forgiven, beautiful, and filled with Him and His glory. God is calling us into His glory, and sin is robbing us of that calling. I'm not saying forgiveness is an easy path; I'm just saying it's the best path.

It should come as no surprise that forgiving my parents of the pain of their divorce would be the first fortress I had to demolish. I was wounded in my heart during that time. The lack of communication and the natural self-centeredness from me only fed into my anger and distrust while growing up. I desperately wanted my dad and mom to ask for my forgiveness and take responsibility for my pain. However, I discovered I was responsible for my own emotional health. I remember a specific night, when I called my dad, not desiring an explanation from him this time, but only to offer forgiveness for my bitterness and anger over the years. I had not been the picture of a good daughter either. This was the scripture that sealed it for me,

"For if you forgive others their trespasses (their reckless and willful sins), your heavenly Father will also forgive you. But if you do not forgive others (nurturing your hurt and anger with the result that it interferes with your relationship with God), then your Father will not forgive your trespasses."
Matthew 6:14–15 (AMP)

There were a lot of tears over the phone that night. Though the miles separated us physically, I began to feel a closeness with my dad I had not felt in years. This evening on the phone with my father was completely different. The tears were cleansing this time. Neither of us was angry at each other anymore. My dad and I both had tender hearts, and I believed he hated the great divide between just us as I did. Neither of us knew how to fix it, but God did. God knows the recipe for health and healing. If we trust him, he will lead us to the righteous path. Yes, forgiveness was my first step in allowing God to be the Lord of my life. Little did I know that I would need to forgive more and more as I grew older. Christ used my dad and our fractured relationship to help heal my heart and then my marriage years later.

If your wounds are deep like mine, you might consider talking to someone. I have seen a counselor, and I am so grateful for the experience. It was the best thing Mark and I did for our marriage and our emotional well-being.

Our counselor gave us tools on how to communicate, unpack our baggage, and heal. God used her mightily. Just for the record, I went to counseling a couple of months before Mark joined me on the journey. It's okay to go first. Mention to your spouse that you are getting coaching. For whatever reason, that term sounds better to them than counseling.

Life can be hard. God is not. He is for you!

With the blessing of my husband, the pastor, I write about our personal journey. This is our story of surviving betrayal and the secrets of pornography in the pulpit.

We all know the enemy seeks to kill, steal and destroy (John 10:10). I believe he is an opportunist and he doesn't mind waiting for the perfect time to lay a trap. Usually, the trap is laid early in our childhood. So, in order to move forward, we had to look back. We all must if we want abundance in life. Our families and generations past are like a blueprint to us and our future. We are destined to follow it if we don't break the patterns of the blueprint. The blessings and the sins of our families go back three to four generations and impact who we are today (Exodus 20:4-6).

What just about wrecked our marriage were the lies and betrayal BUT also my response to those things. Emotional trauma in my childhood led to triggers in our marriage. I hated looking back. I believed all things were made new when I accepted Christ as my Savior.

"Therefore, if anyone is in Christ, he is a new
creation: old things have passed away;
behold, all things have become new."
2 Corinthians 5:17 (NKJV)

Period. Drop the mic. This is true. But this is where I got tripped up. Yes, my dead spirit was instantly made new when I accepted Christ. In an instant, old things passed away and all things become new. My spirit man was alive with the power to change me and my future. But my soul man with my emotional baggage and wounds needed to be unpacked and healed. Discipled. Pushing away or moving away from my past did not mean my past had no impact on me. Looking back, I was amazed how much of my past followed me into my present at this point. Generations of brokenness, divorce, adultery, inability to have relationships with other family members, mistrust, were to name of few.

I encourage you to answer the call to go deeper. Let God take you on an adventure. He will refresh and restore your soul. Intimacy with Christ is possible. Walking in wholeness is possible, and discovering your dreams and callings will be a part of it. Don't stop because the journey gets difficult. Learn to hear the voice of the One who spoke you into creation.

"My sheep hear My voice, and I
know them, and they follow Me."
John 10:27 (NKJV)

Follow God, and he will be the light to your path. This is my account of hearing from the Good Shepherd, my good, good Father. There were a lot of twists and turns in my journey to set a heart free from my emotional trauma. Unhealed wounds only open us up to follow our broken blueprints in our family history. I'm thankful for every part of my story, even the painful parts. Because the painful parts led me to the healing parts.

Dear Father,

You know our emotional wounds typically happen early in our lives and have the most impact. Sadly, we are usually ill-equipped to fully understand how to heal them. But I love how you connect the pieces of our lives like a puzzle. Forgiveness is such a huge part of our wholeness. Lord, I pray you would be with my friends now as they embark on a journey of healing. You have not left us stranded. You are a God who is with us. Reveal our emotional wounds that happened early in our lives, so we can see you for who you really are. You are present, and you are with us. And you will never abandon us. I pray you connect every piece of our soul back together and stronger than before. We invite you on this journey. Reveal yourself throughout these pages. Perfect love casts out all fear. Holy Spirit, lead us on this path.

In Jesus Name,

Amen

"What happens to our soul happens to our cells."
Susie Larson. Fully Alive

Don't fear the journey.... God has healing in mind.

We all experience emotional trauma in our lives growing up. Do you know of any wounds or emotional trauma God wants to heal you from? Write them down.

_____

_____

_____

_____

_____

_____

_____

_____

Who do you need to forgive to move forward? Journal it here.

_____

_____

_____

_____

_____

_____

_____

chapter three
It Started
With A Feeling

I am a feeler. I like to connect with people and try to believe the best in others. But the revealing of the emotional affair accompanied by my past emotional baggage exposed the wounds and lies buried deep within my soul. Looking back, it started with a feeling. A gut feeling.

Years have passed since the upheaval, and I started to look back at the pages of my journal during the tumultuous season of our marriage. These pages in my journal were titled "That which was hidden." My remembrance did not hurt as much as I thought it would, even though I remember each feeling vividly. A woman's heart tends to capture feelings like pictures. It is the beauty of a woman's mind how we can recall the details of events with profound accuracy. Yet, the distance of time between me and that which was hidden helped to ease the remembrance of the lingering pain.

Tucked inside my journal dated March 5th, was a weather-beaten faded sticky note with the following scripture I can easily repeat by memory now.

"Fear not for I am with you;
be not dismayed, for I am your God;
I will strengthen you, I will help you,
I will uphold you with my righteous right hand."
Isaiah 41:10 (ESV)

Just three months after God promised me in His Word whatever was hidden he would reveal, was this jewel. Though His promise to strengthen me and be with me was comforting, it did not stop the shaking. I was anxious to leave the house and anxious to stay in the house by myself. I tried to lean on the only thing I knew I could trust, which was God and His Word.

Driving the forty-five minutes to counseling often made me feel anxious as well. I often thought about what would be discovered or if I could handle the truth. The bright pink sticky note was on the dashboard of my car. It was there for many, many months, if not a year, before I placed it inside my journal for safekeeping. I recited this scripture often in response to my life filled with anxiety. I knew I didn't need to be afraid, but I was. I knew these words were penned by the prophet Isaiah to God's people

in exile, but I felt certain it was a handwritten note to me.
A fight or flight feeling was upon me daily during this dark
season. Of the two choices my feelings were offering, flight
became my preferred option most days. There were days I
did not want to leave the house, and then there were days
I had to leave. The sun faded the bright pink sticky note
while God was busy driving the scripture deeper in my
heart.

I began to be fascinated about studying the brain.
Why was I feeling this way? And could I make anxiety
stop? I was desperate to make some sense of my perceived
craziness. I learned the amygdala (two almond-shaped
masses in your brain) is involved with the fear circuit in
your brain. When we are stressed, these glands respond by
pumping the hormone epinephrine into our bloodstream.
Your response when epinephrine is released into your
system is the fight or flight feelings. I definitely had too
much epinephrine in my bloodstream. I was stressed and
my heart felt like it was on overdrive. We had moved to
a new neighborhood less than a year earlier which meant
a new school for our two boys, a new job for Mark and
myself, and new health issues for me. I learned about what
physically happens to your body when you feel anxious, but
at this point I was in the middle of discovering "the why." I
desperately wanted to learn why I felt anxious.

During one of my "flight" moments, before that which

was hidden was revealed, one of my best friends called and suggested we meet up. I was going out that evening to take our youngest son to pick up a gift, so I decided to also meet my friend, Linda, at Cracker Barrel. I remember truthfully explaining the struggle I was experiencing with anxiety. I had not told anyone yet. But I remember telling my friend I wasn't willing to keep living with the intensity of anxiety in my life anymore. I had prayed and desperately wanted God to make these feelings stop. I was unaware at that moment God indeed heard my cry and was sending me help. Linda quietly reached into her purse and pulled out a business card.

"Here you go sister." I looked at it and read Licensed Mental Health Counseling with the doctor's name and phone number scribed in the lower right corner of the card.

"This might be the best gift you can give yourself," my friend said.

Honestly, in the moment, it made me feel more defeated. I was more aware of the stereotype of a licensed mental health counselor then the gift it would be for me. I had racing thoughts of *why can't I hold my life together?*

I have since discovered if God does not remove or change whatever it is, then He wants to teach, reveal, or heal something in our lives.

I held onto the business card for several days, hoping

things would change. Begrudgingly nothing changed, and I felt counseling was my next step. I needed a break from my racing thoughts.

Years ago, I did not want to face anything which made me seem fragile, frail, or in need. Never mind, we are all human, broken, and flawed. From my early years of brokenness, I felt the only way through pain was to be tough and push through or push down my feelings. My heart ached as a young girl. I convinced myself that any feelings of weakness were for sissies. Only to further my resolve regarding my toughness, on one of my milestone birthdays, I was feeling nostalgic. I asked myself questions. Had I become all I desired to be growing up? What did I want to become when I was older?

I called my mom and asked her these two questions. My hopes were somehow I had achieved my childhood goals of becoming tough. My mom laughed and responded, "You wanted to be a cowgirl." My mom chuckled again, and we continued our conversation, "The funny thing about your dream was there was not a tough bone in your body growing up. You have always had a tender heart." I guess I believed having a tender heart equated with being fragile or frail. I have since discovered it was a lie I believed.

I love my tender heart, and I have discovered courage in embracing my tenderness. Tenderness means you are connected to your emotions. If you have a tender heart, don't believe the lie that you are weak. God gave you this heart and these emotions. We are part of him and his image to others. He has used others in scripture, movies, and friends to awaken my heart to this truth. With our tender heart, we feel, we connect, and we love. We have compassion and empathy for others, which is a sign of emotional intelligence.

"Courage is not the absence of fear, but rather the judgment that something else is more important than fear. The brave may not live forever, but the cautious do not live at all. From now on you'll be traveling the road between who you think you are and who you can be. The key is to allow yourself to make the journey." Meg Cabot

This quote along with this scripture,

> *"For God did not give us a spirit of timidity or*
> *cowardice or fear, but (He has given us a spirit)*
> *of power and of love and of sound judgment and*
> *personal discipline (abilities that result in a*
> *calm, well-balanced mind and self control)."*
> *2 Timothy 1:7 (AMP)*

has propelled me to get outside my comfort zone. I desire a journey of health and wholeness, but in order to get there, I needed to face my fears.

With feelings of anxiety at an all-time high, I grabbed

the business card my friend gave me and made the call to Dr. Sandy several days later. I was willing to travel down a road between who I thought I was and who I could be. I learned after a few visits with the counselor I was handed a gift. In fact, I believe God led four women to help me in my journey. Funny, I did not want the stigma of needing a mental health counselor, but when God put together a whole team of women in my corner, it was as if He was choreographing an elaborate symphony for my future healing. Looking back, it was the hardest and the most beautiful thing I had ever experienced.

I remember Dr. Sandy told me upon our first meeting, "My goal for our time together is for you to understand anxiety is a gift for you. It's your internal clock inside letting you know something is out of balance." I had no clue how these horrible feelings could possibly be a gift. However, over the next several months and through her expertise, I began to see a bit clearer. At the time there were still missing pieces to the puzzle, but week by week, we would unpack what I knew. There would be several months before Mark would join me in her office because of the discovery of his emotional affair. And then the layers and secrets began to unfold. As more truth emerged, strangely my anxiety lifted. I was not crazy. Our marriage was a wreck, but I was getting emotionally stronger.

It was difficult to watch nothing be done to correct

the situation at church. Mark was still allowed to lead worship. And we began to hear sermons from the pulpit about accountability and how to safeguard your marital relationships. As far as the other staff member, she was still at church too. I needed to be rescued. Have you ever needed to be rescued? Mark and I needed rescuing for our marriage and from the church. It was a sticky situation. Our livelihood was attached to Mark leading worship every Sunday. I had a difficult time trying to reconcile the man from the pastor. But God was hearing my relentless plea and making a way of escape. An escape from our unhealthy relationship, from the lies, and sadly from the church we were attending. Time and counseling would give us a safe harbor for our secrets to surface. And trust me, there were more secrets to be revealed, but initially, it all started with a feeling.

As our emotional wounds were healing, and as our brokenness was being exposed, God began to teach us. Mark and I have both learned emotional affairs can be just as damaging as physical affairs. **Men connect more physically, and women connect more emotionally.** So, when there has been unfaithfulness in these areas, the wounds can run deeper than we might think. Physical, sexual affairs typically have a small duration whereas emotional connections can live longer. Emotional affairs can unfold into a greater form of betrayal. Research from the American Association for Marriage and Family Therapy reveals the extent of the problem. About 45% of men have reported being drawn into an emotional affair at some point. Emotional affairs can be a slippery slope. Men are quick to justify their behavior as "I did not have sex with another woman" defense. Emotional infidelity does not register as cheating with men. Because of a woman's ability to be emotionally connected to her feelings and to others we love, an emotional affair is typically more difficult for women to overlook. It's painful when a wife feels like her husband is connecting with someone else emotionally. Honestly, our emotions connect us with intimacy. And intimacy is exactly what a couple needs to be connected with each other.

Paradoxically, men are hurt far more if their wife has a physical affair with another man because men connect physically and visually. No matter which spouse, the danger of an emotional affair is it can lead to disconnection from each other. It's difficult to manage two relationships at the same time. Emotional affairs with others typically have a few signs:

1. Sexual rejection from your spouse
2. Less caring from the spouse having the emotional connection
3. High irritability

4. Forgetfulness
5. Often, we don't hear our spouse say, I love you.

I thought I was not giving Mark what he needed emotionally, or somehow, I let him down as a partner. What we have both discovered in our healing process was that our core needs could only be met by God.

Affirmation, security, purpose, and identity are the four basic needs which come only from God if we want to walk in emotional health. Discovering these core needs and where they come from helped us heal. However, there were some dusty roads to travel. I remembered wanting so desperately to be justified and for someone to take my side. I desired someone to pay the price for the pain I had been caused. Our pain defines us only if we let it.

Jesus met the woman from Samaria coming to the well for water personally on her path. Like her, Jesus met me in my real-life Samaria. I didn't have five husbands, but I had "some areas" in my life that needed His Living Water. He will meet you in your "some area" as well. Jesus called out her thirst. I often wonder about the pain or lonely nights she might have cried out to the Messiah to heal her heart. I could relate to the brokenness in her heart. We all can. It's because affirmation, security, purpose, and identity comes only from God . When we try to find these needs in others, we typically are left thirsty.

Think about it. If there are areas of thirst in your life, I invite you to come to the well. Christ will surely satisfy you there. He will affirm you. He will cover you, and give you security. He will speak purpose into your core being, and He will place His identity upon you.

Are you thirsty? Jesus is coming to your Samaria. I hope these pages will be a type of well for you. Don't substitute your thirst for an easy relief. Once He fills the void places within, His Living Water in you will become a jar for others. He will surely meet you at the driest place in your life. He will give you a fresh encounter.

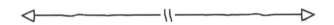

But whoever drinks the water

I give them will never thirst.

Indeed, the water I give them will

become in them a spring of water

welling up to *eternal life.*

John 4:14 (NIV)

Dear Father,

The enemy is so good at lying to us. Just like he did to the woman in Samaria. The enemy has no good thoughts towards us. He whispers lies that you are not trustworthy. That you are not a good father and are not for us. Those are all lies. Teach us about the areas we need your healing. Help us to hear you more clearly. Train our spirit that you are for us. You use disappointments in life to draw us to you. Increase our faith to be brave and to be courageous. When we enter territory we have never seen before, remind us, like you did Joshua, to not be afraid, nor be dismayed, for YOU are with us wherever we go. Falling in love with my spouse was so much fun, but falling in love with you was an adventure. Show us our next step. Show us our counterfeits where we have substituted affirmation, security, purpose, and identity for someone or something else. We need your living water. Fill our thirst.

Amen

Write down where you are thirsty for Jesus to meet
you.

_____

_____

_____

_____

_____

_____

_____

_____

Which core need do you need most from God:
affirmation, security, purpose, or identity? Journal it here.

_____

_____

_____

_____

_____

_____

_____

_____

_____

THE BEAUTIFUL UGLY TRUTH

chapter four

Pornography in the Pulpit

Weeks turned into months and months of counseling. Some days were filled with good conversations, and some days were quiet, numb days. Most days, I felt alone in the fight. Who was I going to confide in about our real issues? Everyone loved and supported Pastor Mark. I would watch and just scratch my head as he led the congregation into the presence of God during a worship service. I honestly felt alone in this season of our marriage and ministry. My only saving grace was our counselor. The days I thought I couldn't continue on, both my counselor and scripture would give me direction on what to do next.

I wanted to get past our nightmare. Honestly, there were some days I just wanted to get past five o'clock without something else blowing up in my face. However, after Mark joined me in counseling, I still couldn't get past that gnawing feeling there was more to our story. I could not explain the feeling. Mark and I were trying to reconnect, but there was something in his eyes that told me otherwise. The only thing I knew to do during this season was to put one foot in front of the other and pray. God was close to my broken heart during this time. Some days, I was scared of what more there could be but I was also determined. I guess it was here, in the valley of suck, that I felt directed to go on another fast.

I wasn't sure how many days I was going to fast or what I was going to fast from. I prayed a lot during this time. Talking to God was the only thing that brought me some kind of comfort. I had not made a concrete decision on the next time I would fast, but I just had a feeling I would. I remember reading the scriptures in 1 Kings 19:5-8. It was about the prophet Elijah. He had just won a victory against the 800 false prophets of Baal. And then he encountered Queen Jezebel. His first battle was a huge victory, but this was just the beginning. I hated reading that part, because I related in some strange way. I felt Mark and I had won a victory, but it was just the beginning for us also.

The prophet had slayed the false prophets and ran from an angry Queen Jezebel.

> *"And he lay down and slept under the broom tree. And*
> *behold, an angel touched him and said to him, "Arise*
> *and eat." And he looked, and behold, there was at his*

head a cake baked on hot stones and a jar of water.
And he ate and drank and lay down again. And the
angel of the LORD came again the second time and
touched him and said, "Arise and eat, for the journey
is too great for you." And he arose and ate and drank,
and went in the strength of that food forty days and
forty nights to Horeb the mount of God."
I Kings 19: 5-8 (ESV)

In this passage, Elijah had just won an amazing battle against the false prophets of Baal. Queen Jezebel threatened to kill the prophet in the same way he had killed her false prophets. Why is it after a great victory, fear has a way of following us? So, Elijah ran and found himself in the wilderness hungry and exhausted. Just as the angel touched Elijah and said, "Arise and eat for the journey is too great for you," somehow I felt God encouraged me to do the same. The journey would be too great in my own strength. I needed to regain strength, but for what? I felt I was good to eat and drink for a week, but I also understood, I would be fasting again, this time for forty days.

I remember asking Mark, "Is there anything else you need to tell me?" His initial response was he had already told me everything. I chose to trust the counseling process, but not Mark.

Mark was encouraged by our counselor and another friend to get it all out on the table. I remember our counselor saying, nothing hurts worse than traveling the road to restoration and rebuilding trust only to find out there were more lies. He was saying there was nothing else hidden, but even with his reassurance, I could not get away from the feeling I was going into another fast.

The wounds of what led us to counseling a month earlier was like a fresh cut trying to heal. If more was going to be exposed, I needed God and his strength for this part of the journey. So, with the heaviest of hearts and a lump in the throat, I decided privately I would fast for more truth.

I still had my daily reminder on the bright pink sticky note. It gave me great comfort during this upheaval.

Looking back, I could not have walked through those days ahead without the strength of God. I could not have imagined or prepared myself, but God knew. Several weeks after "D-Day" #1 (the first confrontation), "D-Day" #2 was upon us. It was another discovery day.

Mark and I had started meeting again on Wednesday nights, just the two of us this time. We would go out to dinner after dropping the kids off at a youth group. Our counselor recommended a book to read called, *His Needs, Her Needs* by William F. Harley Jr. We would underline what was pertinent to us in each chapter and then meet weekly to discuss each chapter.

This week, chapter four was about how men are stimulated visually and the pornography industry is banking on this fact. I underlined the sentence with no expectation of its significance. We had just finished eating dinner at a barbecue restaurant nearby the church, and started going over our notes. I looked at Mark after we read over this section and I asked him one simple question, "Is this true?"

Mark gave me an answer which caught me completely off guard. The truth was busy setting us free, but I was certainly not prepared for this answer. "Yes," he said. I remember being stunned by his acknowledgment, not about men being stimulated visually, but the acknowledgment that he was susceptible to this temptation. I knew he was a man, but he was also a pastor who I believed had safeguarded himself from the evil hook of pornography. "You have preached about this," I said. And then, I began asking him specific questions.

"Magazines?"

"Yes"

"Internet?"

"Yes"

At this point, I felt betrayed all over again. My words came stumbling out my mouth quicker than my brain could engage.

"How deep into the internet?"

"What kind of pornography?"

"Have you been in chat rooms?"

"Did you talk with anyone?"

"No no no no," he initially responded.

I remember getting up from the table with no announcement and walking out to the car. We still had time before we went to pick up our boys, but I was finished talking and stunned by the truth of this unwelcome news. I felt sucker-punched in my stomach and the tears began to flow. I guess Mark was paying our dinner bill inside the restaurant. I was standing by the car, shocked. We had just started talking again and trying to rebuild our marriage only to discover that there were more secrets. It was amazing how quickly my anger rose to the surface again. Here we were, back to the beginning of the betrayal I felt several weeks ago. He met me at the car and opened my locked door. It seemed as though he wanted to say something. I just remember saying before he had a chance, "I do not want to hear anything else you have to say right now." I was stunned and terrified at what more he had to add to the story. I did not want an apology or any more details at this point.

My mind began racing with thoughts in the silent ride back to pick up our boys from church. Who was I married to? How do you compete with these fantasies and their bodies? I had birthed our children. My body showed signs of that truth. *Oh my goodness, our children* I thought. I was heartbroken for them. Their dad was their hero. Even though I knew Mark wanted to say more, I had let the quietness fill the car. I prayed silently God would protect our boys during this upheaval. I also prayed I could hold my emotions together in front of the boys.

The night was long, and the silence was filled with thousands of questions in my mind. I thought we were on the other side of our mess. The realization of being deceived once again was painful. Pornography. Seriously? Not only was he my husband, but he was also a pastor. The scariest thing about deception is you don't know you are being deceived. God has to reveal the truth. I am not sure how I kept from lashing out every emotion I was feeling that evening. Sometimes in the moment, being shocked and feeling numb is a gift from God. I learned when you don't know what to say, don't say anything.

Once again, I woke up the next morning only to realize the nightmare was still going on. I did what I needed to do to get the boys ready for school and out the door. The conversation between Mark and I was tense. I was seething. He came into the bathroom with his hands held up saying, "I am telling you this time, this is everything."

I retorted, "Don't say anything because I don't believe a word you are saying." I angrily told him to get out of the bathroom and to call one of his friends or call Doctor

Sandy. Whoever he thought he could be honest with and get out all his secrets this time. I remember stepping out of the bathroom to see Mark outside on his phone. I hoped he was finally telling someone the truth. I looked to see Mark rubbing his forehead.

When Mark came back inside that morning , he asked me if I would come with him to church. He was still on staff and had to pastor other hurting souls amidst our own grief and revelation. I was still shocked by the information but knowing there could be more he needed to talk about, I agreed to go with him. We went by the church office for a few things, and then stopped for lunch. We tried to have a conversation over lunch, but it was awkward. He told me he just wanted to be with me. He wanted more time to decompress from the night before, so I suggested maybe a walk in the park.

We arrived at the neighborhood park and walked quietly around. Honestly, I had nothing to say. Mark and I had been having some of our most difficult conversations in our seventeen years of marriage these past few months. I did not know what to say, and I was confident silence was my best option. As we began to walk the trail we discovered under the trees and by the water a bench. I thought it would be a quiet peaceful place for us to sit. We started the conversation with non-descriptive questions and answers about our surroundings. I was answering his questions until he ran out of things to tell me. We paused and sat in silence for a moment. "I have more to tell you," he said.

I can remember taking the deepest breath, pausing as though it seemed like forever until I could exhale. My heart sank. I was not sure what he was going to say next. With my eyes deeply hidden behind my sunglasses, he began to reveal the depths of his pornography addiction. All the questions he previously said no to the night before, he began to answer in detail. My heart sank more. It was like I could audibly hear the breaking of my fragile heart. My bloodshot eyes began to fill, and nothing held back the tears. I kept thinking, *no this can't be true! This is not my Mark. This could not be us.* I silently applauded his truthfulness, but it did not lessen the blow. I felt ripped apart. I was shocked, numb, and a little bit more broken. I could not find any words to respond back to him. With tears flowing down my face quicker than I could wipe them away, I told him I was ready to go. I was ready to go back to a rented house that was not ours. We had just moved our family to Tampa eighteen months earlier for this? We walked back to the car without a word and were home in a few short minutes.

We walked into the house and I went straight into the bathroom I had left earlier that morning. I closed the bathroom door and began to get sick to my stomach. I was literally sickened by the truth. The deception. The lies. This virtual world had invaded our marriage. Mark knocked on the door and asked if there was anything he could do. My response was quick and stern, "You have done enough. I need you to go away." I cried and cried while I lay on the cold floor. I was heartsick by the loss of our once sweet, naive relationship. I had known our relationship was in trouble for some time, but the light of the emotional affair and pornography was more than I felt my heart could take.

When I knew my stomach was empty, I knew it was safe to come outside the bathroom. I walked into the kitchen and over to the refrigerator. I got a glass of water, picked up my cell phone, and walked right out the front door. I wasn't sure where I was going; I just knew I had to leave. I left my keys, so my feet were my only mode of transportation. I walked and walked and walked. I called my friend in Georgia and continued to walk some more. She listened graciously at my angry tirade as I described how furious I was at this point. I simply did not know who I was married to anymore. I must have walked the block four or five times with my hands waving in the air, finding all kinds of descriptive words for my raw emotions while I cried. How was this my life?

Once I caught my breath from the tirade, and I was confident I said everything, my friend told me she supported me and would do anything for me. I asked her to pray for me. I was able to say good-bye to her and hang up the phone. I continued to walk some more to try and make sense of how this day had unfolded. I had never felt grief like this before. The one my heart had trusted all those years had actually broken it with his lies and betrayal. At this moment, I was sure I was done. I did not see any way to repair what was shattered, but God could.

I continued to beat a path around the block. My phone rang and it was Dr. Sandy. I answered the phone confident that Mark had asked her to call me. I answered, "Hello Dr. Sandy," not giving her a chance to say hello back to me. "Did Mark call you?" And to my surprise she simply said, "No." She went on to ask me what was going on. I asked a second time if Mark had called. "So, if Mark didn't call you, then why are you calling me?" One thing I know about doctors is they typically don't call you. Actually, she never called us. We always called her to set up our next appointments. I will never forget her answer in that fateful moment. She said these words, "The Holy Spirit told me to call you today at this moment to check on you. Can you tell me what is going on?"

I began to cry all over again. I took a deep breath and tried to explain the past several hours of our day. I probably cussed as I muddled through every emotion and event of the day. I kept walking and talking, walking and talking. I finally landed on my neighbor's bench right beside our house to wrap up the end of our long conversation.

She began giving me her counselor's advice after all my ranting. "Obviously, Mark trusts you with the deepest secrets of his life, and at some point, you need to give him another safe place to land." *Give him a safe place to land*, I thought. Who will give me a safe place?

She continued, "I am not saying today or tomorrow or even next week, Gwen. You take your time with this one. But at some point, you will have to give him a soft place to land in his emotions. You have already offered this safe place before to him, which is why he felt he could tell you more upon your request. So if you want to continue in this process of restoration and get all the secrets out on the table, I encourage you, in your own timing, to offer him another safe place to land." Then she asked, "Gwen, will you allow me to pray for you and your family?" My defenses always crumble when God is involved in my life. I am not sure when she went from counselor to minister, but in the moment, she made the switch. That prayer was full of God's presence and power. The enemy wanted to kill our marriage and our family, and it looked like he was winning the battle, but God interrupted. God called me that day on the phone and became flesh for me through our counselor. I am confident she would be very humbled by this statement and might even brush it off, but she was Jesus Christ with skin on that day for me and for us.

Please don't miss the power of that information Dr. Sandy provided for me that day.

When you ask for the truth and it comes, you must give your spouse a safe place to land.

Somehow through her prayer and God's power, I walked back into the house I had stormed out of earlier. It was a critical moment. I remember walking in and looking into Mark's eyes. His eyes were bloodshot red. I could only assume he had been crying. He looked exhausted and scared all at the same time. I had not seen him this way. His eyes looked up at me tenderly, but he did not say a word. We stared at one another for a minute or two. And then I remember asking him if he was okay.

It's been years since this day, and I still remember it so vividly. It could have gone so many different ways, but Dr. Sandy's voice kept saying in my memory, "Give him a safe place to land." The words, "are you okay?" sounded strange coming out of my mouth. I was angry. Honestly, I didn't even know if I was okay. And yet, I heard those words coming out of my mouth before I had time to think about what I was really saying. I saw something in Mark that I had never seen before. He was sitting on the sofa, looking up at me. His tears and terror softened my heart. All he said was, "No, I am not okay." I walked over to the sofa where he was sitting, and I sat down beside him. I remember telling him I didn't need him to be perfect, just truthful. I believe God took over in that moment. I remember wrapping my arms around his shoulders and pulling him over onto my lap. Mark later described this moment as pivotal. He says, as he lay there, he felt God go to the root of his soul and pull out all the secrets. The root of all his denial, the root of him not measuring up, and all the ways he had considered himself less than. It was a surreal, sacred moment where God took over.

"Sometimes a sacred moment of grace does not feel like grace in the moment." Mark said this statement years later as he spoke about all the denial we had survived. God was with Mark and me during this gut-wrenching season. It was His grace. God's grace didn't feel like grace in that moment, but looking back, it's exactly what it was. Grace. The term "sacred moments" refers to brief periods of time when people experience spiritual qualities of transcendence, ultimacy, boundlessness, interconnectedness, and spiritual emotions. I had asked Mark for the truth multiple times. I had asked God to heal our marriage multiple times. And God was answering my prayers in a way I could not have imagined.

It was a turning point for both of us that day. We share this story often now in ministry settings and with other couples. We speak of how God's grace (not me) walked back in the door that day. It is a special day neither of us will ever forget and a day that changed both of our lives.

God met both of us in our living room individually and as a couple. We talked, we cried, and we both shared how we felt.

God showed up as our protector, and our true Father. The Holy Spirit came as our healer and comforter, and Christ came to this earth as our payment. We are quick to judge a situation or someone else's shortcomings, sin, failure, or points of missing the mark. But Christ was our payment for sin. Christ represents our righteousness. Only looking back could I see this picture clearly. God's grace walked me back into the house to be a part of something nothing short of miraculous. If we are willing to allow the truth to surface and offer a safe place for each other to land, God can do the miraculous.

Critical moments like these might be different from your story, but God is still the same. He will meet you in your moment. In your most heart-wrenching, difficult season, God will be with you. He will walk you through every circumstance. I wish I could say from that moment on, everything was better for Mark and me, but there was still more to our journey. We got a taste of truth. The moment was not easy, but that moment strangely brought with it relief. Truth showed up in our relationship to give us something to build upon. That which was hidden had finally given way to the light of a new day.

I understand the truth can be painful, but it is the

truth that sets you free. It was this truth which became our building block. I encourage you to be truthful with yourself and be truthful with others. Nothing can be built on a faulty foundation, not:

- A building
- A marriage
- A family
- A friendship
- A business

> *"Unless the Lord builds the house,*
> *those who built it, labor in vain."*
> Psalm 127:1 (ESV)

No matter how beautiful the outward construction may seem to the normal eye, without a firm foundation it is only a matter of time before destruction is imminent. Much like our lives, if we are not truthful, eventually cracks in our foundation will only lead to more destruction. God will be your shield. Let truth reign so truth will heal you. Without the foundation of truth, you have nothing to build upon. I cannot express this enough. As difficult and gut-wrenching the truth was for us, it was the very thing we needed to be exposed so we could heal. There is a powerful passage in God's living word,

"If you abide in my word, you are truly my disciples, and you will know the truth, and the truth will set you free."
John 8:32 (ESV)

Let God's truth of who He is and His love for you set you free. Be courageous. Be fearless. Be forgiving. Pornography is a silent force that destroys families.

An enemy silently came into our house and wreaked havoc on our marriage and our sex life. Not Mark. And the worse part of it was discovering I felt all alone in this. Who could I tell? Who has walked through this before?

My husband, the pastor, was secretly drawn to pornography. I wanted help, but did not feel comfortable telling anyone at the church our secret. I began to understand the draw to pornography didn't start when Mark became a pastor. The hook of porn captured him at a young age. As we sat on our sofa crying, I remember asking Mark how we would be able to walk through this. I wondered if other couples had walked through this and survived. I knew we had a counselor we could physically talk to about this, but who else was brave enough to tell their story? There were more questions than answers for months and I felt all alone in the process. I guess I was naive to think other pastors and their wives hadn't walked through this nightmare. I just wanted guidance. I wanted to know someone had made it to the other side of their destruction. I wanted to be a couple who had survived.

As weeks turned into months, I was shocked to find how many others had walked this path. I remember talking about it with our counselor. She seemed happy with our progress, but the more we talked about it with her, the more my anger lay on the surface. I was going through the stages of grief but there had been no funeral. Stages of betrayal are just like stages of grief: shock, denial, anger (obsession), bargaining, depression (mourning), and acceptance.

We discovered the power of Mark's struggle with pornography was in the secret. When we told others, the secret of it lost its power. If you have experienced the pain of the virtual breach of pornography, there is hope. If your spouse struggles with pornography, there is hope. You are not alone in this battle.

The statistics on viewing pornographic material through online devices are astounding. I remember sitting in Dr. Sandy's office and she said to us both, "When you guys get the victory in this, you will be able to help so many people. The pastors I see in my office dealing with the issue of pornography are staggering. I would go as far to say this is an epidemic." She was not lying.

The more I have studied the effects and the percentages of online users, the more my heart breaks. Mark has shared our story on many retreats and small group settings. Inevitably, after the meetings, their wives come up to me explaining their same heartbreak.

I have had wives secretly ask me these questions.

"How do I compete with online activities? I look nothing like these ladies.

"How did you rebuild trust?"

"What if he does it again?"

These are just a few of the questions I am asked frequently.

"Pornography does not have a demographic anymore, it goes across all demographics," said Paul Fishbein, Founder of Adult View News.

As I mentioned, it entered our world years prior, before I knew Mark or anything about its destruction. Mark had been exposed to it as a young teenager far before I entered into his life. The memory of those pictures does not go away, he said to me one day. It's a battle of constantly taking every thought captive. Exposed at a young age, guys grow into men, and the battle ensues for their purity and mind. Pornography can affect men who are executives, business owners, Christians, and non-Christians alike. Even pastors are not immune to this draw. Thankfully, God has promised a way of escape. However, to not be aware of its pull would be like an ostrich sticking its head in the sand. Sadly, the statistics show pornography does not just affect men anymore.

An article provided through Covenant Eyes had these statistics. (www.covenanteyes.com/pornstat/)

- 51% of pastors said they struggle with the temptation.
- 64% of Christian men and 15% of Christian women view pornography at least once a month.
- 75% of pastors admitted to not making themselves accountable to anyone.

This statistic breaks my heart. I remember Mark telling me, "Who was I going to be accountable to? I was the pastor on staff." I think his greatest fear was not only the thought of me finding out, but also his job as a pastor being in trouble. Our entire livelihood was attached to this secret. Pornography thrives on secrecy. Church members and pastors feel trapped in the sin and shame of it. One of the saddest statistics I came across in this article was this one.

Those who self-identify as "fundamentalists" are 91% more likely to look at porn than those who are not.

One in five Google searches on mobile devices is for pornography. One in eight online searches is on a computer.

Because of its effect on marriages, The American Academy of Matrimonial Lawyers reports 56% of divorce cases involve one party having "an obsessive interest in pornographic websites." It destroys marriages and slowly erodes one's soul, male or female. Pornography, without hope in Christ, kills intimacy. It tears down a couple's sex life and diminishes trust, but also creates a lack of attraction to the family and child-raising.

Though the statistics for viewing pornography are lower for women, it still has entered their world.

Recent studies show 31% of women watch porn every week.

30% of women view it a few times a month and 10% of women admit to viewing it daily. It's not just men who watch porn anymore. The internet has made it so accessible. Women admit to watching on their own, but most women (96%) have watched with a partner and says it "improves" sex. It may seem like it does for a moment, but studies show after prolonged exposure to pornography it slowly makes it impossible for men to perform with their spouse.

Of hundreds of college students surveyed:

- 93% of boys said they were exposed to porn before the age of 18.
- 62% of girls said they were exposed to porn before the age of 18.
- 64% of college boys and 18% of college women spend time online for internet sex every week.

- 15% of boys and 9% of girls (under the age of 18) have seen pornography.
- 32% of boys and 18% of girls have seen bestiality online.
- 39% of boys and 23% of girls have seen sexual bondage online.
- 83% of boys and 57% of girls have seen group sex online.
- 69% of boys and 55% of girls have seen same-sex intercourse online.

80% of pornography that floods the world is rated as "hardcore porn." When most of us think of porn, it's "soft porn." Hardcore porn includes pornography as seen in the list above, but not limited to, and it's entering into the world of our children.

I know these stats are disturbing. My heart sinks writing them, but let these stats empower you to know the truth. I would not have known to ask Mark the questions about pornography if I had not been reading the book *His Needs, Her Needs.*

The truth has brought us closer together as a couple. Victory does not come unless we are willing to expose the enemy who is after our loved ones. On days I was sure I could not go forward, our counselor encouraged me with the strength of God's Word and reminded me I asked God for the truth. I did ask God for the truth, and in all of the upheaval, He brought me exactly what I needed.

I remember one day walking into our counselor's office, Dr. Sandy handed me an index card with this scripture penned on it,

"When I passed by you again and saw you, behold, you were at the age of love, and I spread the corner of my garment over you and covered your nakedness; I made my vow to you and entered into a covenant with you, declares the Lord God, and you became mine."
Ezekiel 16:8 (ESV)

It was true; I felt the most vulnerable during that time, exposed and naked. Could everybody else see it? And in the moment of vulnerability, I felt God's presence cover me. That is what His Word does. It strengthens us, covers us, comforts us, and speaks truth right in the middle of our storms in life.

The enemy is not your spouse. We are wrestling against principalities in high places. Ephesians 6 encourages us to equip ourselves with the Armor of God. God has given us weapons.

Interesting enough, even though pornography had its hook in Mark, it was not the root of our problems. We discovered pornography, or any other sin, was like a leaf on a tree. We had to be willing to excavate the root system to see what was driving these lies and producing fruit. We all have experienced wounds early on in our lives. Our emotions and personalities are forming up to the age of ten. As mentioned earlier, <u>we all have four basic needs for acceptance, security, purpose, and identity.</u> When we look to people other than the Creator to fulfill those needs, we typically are left in need. Only the Creator can satisfy His creation.

Once the lies and deceptions were exposed, the healing process began for us. Be willing to communicate, to be a safe place for one another. Pray for your spouse. Pray for your children. And I will pray God protects your heart if you are on this journey.

Dear Jesus,

Thank you for loving us right where we are at. Be with us like you promised and lead us out of the darkest places. Expose any darkness to the Light of who you are. Let the truth of your love for us set us free to breathe again. You have so much more for us. I know you have promised us life and life more abundantly. Thank you for defeating the darkness seeking after us. I'm so thankful for the finished work of Christ Jesus. I have read the end of our story, we win! Thank you for paying the price for us to walk in victory. No longer slaves to fear. Create in us Trees of Righteousness. Let our root system be strong, so when the storms arrive, we will be safe and secure in all your promises.

In Jesus Name,
Amen

Who do you need to give a safe place to land? Journal here.

_____

_____

What secrets do you need to share with your spouse?

_____

_____

THE BEAUTIFUL UGLY TRUTH

chapter five

From Restoration to Reformation

Restoration is a choice. We each have a choice to make. I had a choice to make. In the middle of choices being made for me and our marriage, I still felt blind-sided. I felt paralyzed emotionally. I discovered we go through stages when decisions are being made without our knowledge. I learned betrayal has stages just like grief. We have lost something. Because of this, we walk through shock, denial, anger, bargaining, depression, testing, and acceptance. It is vital we identify each stage and give the stage its proper expression.

I remember when Mark and I were going through our upheaval. I was afraid of the process of grief and that certain stages would overtake me. I studied about grief and read other authors' writings. In doing so, I believe there is one more stage that needs to be added to the process of grief after acceptance. It is significance. There is significance for your suffering. There is a reason. We just need the courage to discover it.

In the 1946 classic book *Man's Search for Meaning*, author Viktor Frankl chronicles his experience as a prisoner in Nazi concentration camps during World War II. There are too many quotes in his writings relating to suffering. I could not imagine his misery, but he gives us all permission to look for significance in our sorrow. And in our personal sufferings, we give others the permission to have the courage to look for significance in their suffering.

He quotes, "When we are no longer able to change a situation, we are challenged to change ourselves."

What if the dark night of our soul is really a blessing? I know in the middle of the darkness, we cannot imagine darkness as a blessing. I often ponder now what my counselor told me the first day we met. She said I would discover anxiety would be a gift for me. I can see clearer now. Maybe she was right.

But have you noticed in the dark, bitter, winter nights of our souls, we ask ourselves these questions:

- Who are we?
- How did we get here?
- How soon will this pass?
- Does God really love me at all?

We usually question God and our purpose when we cannot see in the darkness. And God is typically silent during this time. We are left alone with these questions. For me, the dark night was the betrayal in our marriage. But betrayal can take on many forms as I have previously mentioned. It could be a divorce or a church split, a job loss, brokenness with other family members, a health crisis, financial issues, a miscarriage, or having your dreams unfulfilled.

There were a few days God spoke clearly to my heart and our situation, but more often, there were days when the silence was deafening. Mark and I would have good days during the healing process, but we had just as many, if not more, difficult days. Most of the journey, I just had to hold on to the last piece of truth Mark had given me. It didn't stop me from crying out frequently. When I would cry out during those days of uncertainty and God felt silent, it was a challenge to stay focused and not wallow in self-pity.

The waiting for God's direction was hard yet very important. Even though trust in our marriage was being re-built, patience and time didn't feel like a friend. I understood without faith it is impossible to please God (Hebrews 11:1), but in desperate times I just needed to know God was with me in the battle. It seemed like weeks turned into months on this uncharted journey. Would the truth really set us free? I needed the reassurance of my Father God. I pleaded with Christ in prayer to say something to my soul.

Alone again at the house one particular day, I cried out in prayer once again to God, "Why won't you say something…anything? Father, please say something," and I would wait to hear, but there was only silence. Have you ever heard the silence? I would busy myself with daily activities, but the ache in my heart would remind me of the only One who could heal. The videotapes in my head from the last counseling session would not relent. And in the silence, my desperate heart would cry out. I remember specifically one day coming out of our kitchen…. alone. I cried out frequently for His presence to relieve my pain. My heart was heavy this particular day, and I remember looking out into our back yard from our large sliding glass door. Our backyard faced many houses on our cul-de-sac. Typically, you could hear kids' laughter and watch some type of outdoor game in our neighborhood, but this time of day all the kids were at school. Questions began to pierce my loneliness. What if my life would be filled with nothing? I was so afraid of being alone. I didn't want my children to suffer the same fate. I remember blurting out to God, "What have I done so bad that you would turn your back on me…why won't you say something?"

This time, I heard His voice inside me. It was louder than the silence. I heard His gentle response back to me, "My Son felt the same way on the cross before His greatest day of victory. Can you trust in me during this dying process? I have a great victory in mind for you. I allow death to come to everything. And where people lose hope is when they see death, and they think that it is over. But I am a God of Resurrection, Gwen. Will you stick around for the Resurrection of these things in your life?"

I am not sure how long I lay on the floor and cried. I felt angst and peace all at the same time. How was that possible? I heard Him speak. He had victory in mind for me. And I learned something at that moment.

God's power is still released even in His silence or presumed absence in our lives.

We die little mini deaths throughout our life, and God loves us and never stops moving. If we let Him, He will reform us. We have a choice to turn our suffering into significance. God had much to teach me.

Even though I felt as if I was dying on the outside…I began to live again on the inside. **The death of something is really the birthing of something else.** God is just clearing the old landscape. In order for something new to grow, God must clear the field for new seeds. Embracing my dark night opened up new ground for the planting. I was a blank slate.

God is amazing in His wisdom and perfect in His timing. Even when a heart is in pain, He still works. He is working especially in the silence. Love has many characteristics. Love is patient. Love suffers long. Love is kind. Love does not demand. Love is not rude. God's heart is for us and wants to restore and reform us.

God was teaching me in my greatest darkness I could trust Him. It was a difficult process for me because of my lack of trust in others. Challenges only propel us and change us if we let them. I had to lay down my right to be right. I was convinced if I behaved well, tithed and said my prayers, I would be in the line of blessings. Christ and his love came and covered me and Mark. Grace covered us both. For every penalty of sin there was a payment. Christ was our covering and our payment. How could I judge, knowing my past. But how could I forgive knowing my present.

Paul, a prisoner of Christ, stated:

"So we do not lose heart. Though our outer self is wasting away, our inner self is being renewed day by day. For this light momentary affliction is preparing for us an eternal weight of glory beyond all comparison, as we look not to the things that are seen but to the things that are unseen. For the things that are seen are transient, but the things that are unseen are eternal."
II Corinthians 4:16-18 (ESV)

You may feel your outward man is perishing, but take

heart, in this place your inward man is being renewed.

By trade, I am an Interior Designer. I have watched pieces of old furniture be stripped down from layers and layers of paint and returned to their former conditions. I also love, metaphorically, what restoration means to us when God takes us from our broken, old condition and restores us anew. But I could not get away from the fact that God was doing something deeper in Mark and me than restoration. And from this pain, we wanted more than our "former condition." What was beyond restoration? What I believed about myself, our marriage, life, church, scriptures, all began to be challenged. The Holy Spirit became my teacher and I was going to school.

While we were being stripped away, I was hungry to know God's Word and why I believed what I believed. I was an empty vessel longing to be filled again. Mark and I would take one step forward and a dozen steps back. I wanted us to move past our pain, but in order to do so, God needed to reform my old ways of thinking. Old patterns of thinking included what I believed about God, about Mark, and about myself. I tried to stay out of my head most days. Often, when my head and heart were heavy, I would go shopping. I call it "retail therapy." I thought I was just venturing out to be by myself, away from my thoughts and our current situation. But God lives within us. Where I go, He is with me. I will never forget the moment. I weaved in and out of the aisles of the Ross store, finding myself in the home decor department. There it was. I stood there in their aisle with a small plaque in my hand crying. I am sure to others it was a strange sight, but to me…it was life. Engraved in the plaque were the words written from I Corinthians 13:7 (ESV):

> *"Love bears all things, believes all things,*
> *hopes all things, endures all things…*
> *Love never fails."*

Could I describe our relationship with this truth from the plague? Maybe not, at least not this particular day. I was confronted by this scripture. Memories of our wedding day came flooding back. We had this scripture read at our wedding, along with saying our vows. For richer or poorer, in sickness and health, for better or worse, till death do us part, we committed to a covenant with each other on our wedding day. How did we travel so far? Those words sounded so poetic.

I am not saying Mark and I were not in love at this point, but the circumstances of our lives came along to test it. I knew in my own power I did not have the strength or courage to actually do these things. My wounds were deep and I still had issues. It felt impossible for this passage to be demonstrated in our lives. I was not sure how my love would suffer long, be kind, not behave rudely, not seek my own way, and not be provoked. But my teacher was teaching me something.

As I stood there with this passage in my hand, all I could see were all the ways in which I had miserably failed this love test. I was not kind, I behaved rudely, I sought my own way, and I was definitely provoked. So, there I stood. I was hoping not in my circumstances, but for God to show up and do the miraculous again. It was a battle between my flesh and my spirit standing in the aisle of the store. I knew the right response God wanted me to have, but my flesh still wanted to be justified. I was not done being hurt, and I silently argued with my Teacher. I was not done grieving. I asked myself, "If I purchased this plaque would it communicate to Mark I was letting him off the hook?" I honestly wanted Mark to pay a little bit more. However, I discovered when I let Mark off my hook, I was actually putting him on God's hook. It was at this place when I decided to hand everything over to God and get out of the way. When I gave the justice of the situation over to the One who can change our circumstances, Christ began to heal both our hearts.

Often, we hold people captive for their wrong-doings by not forgiving them. However, it's amazing what God can do when we get out of His way. There was a collision of Old Testament and New Testament going on in my head with two spiritual truths in battle as I held that plaque in Ross. First collision was the Old Testament Law that required a penalty for sin. The law was the hook wanting to be justified. I unknowingly desired someone other than Christ to pay a debt for Mark's sin. We do this when we choose not to forgive.

Ask the woman who was caught in the act of adultery in John 8. The Pharisees, (the law) demanded she should be stoned. But Christ (grace) set her free on the dusty road. The law demanded payment. Christ paid it. God can point out to us when our theology needs adjusting. How often do we ask for grace, but do not extend it?

So, I purchased that darn plaque as a reminder of how God met me and healed me. As I drove home and had some quiet time, the thought came to me. It took the most intimate relationship, our marriage, and its failure to teach me such a valuable, life-changing truth. I tried to accomplish good works to have a place with God. I tried to earn favor through my action, my tithe, and my service. **The harsh reality was, I could let love win or I could be justified and lose.** This moment for me was about a good collision of grace and the law. One of the two would win out. Did I want the Law to win or did I want Grace to win? You can live by the law or you can live by grace. At this crossroads in our marriage, I discovered,

The Law always demands and Grace always covers.

Galatians 3:10-13 (AMP) says it this way:

"For all who depend on the Law (seeking justification and salvation by obedience to the Law and the observance of rituals) are under a curse; for it is written, 'Cursed (condemned to destruction) is everyone who does not abide by all things written in the book of the Law, so as to practice them?" Now it is clear that no one is justified (that is, declared free of the guilt of sin and its penalty, and placed in right standing) before God by the Law, for the righteous (the just, the upright) shall live by faith. But the Law does not rest on or require faith (it has nothing to do with faith but instead, the Law) says, 'He who practices them (the things prescribed by the Law) shall live by them (instead of faith).' Christ purchased our freedom and redeemed us from the curse of the Law and its condemnation by becoming a curse for us, for it is written, 'Cursed is everyone who hangs (crucified) on a tree (cross)'--in order that in Christ Jesus the blessing of Abraham might also come to the Gentiles, so that we would all receive (the realization of) the promise of the (Holy) Spirit through faith."

Christ paid our debt of sin. His love and grace heals us. This was just the beginning to a new journey of reformation…a re-formation. Christ's love and His grace was reforming me. I had been a Christian at this point for most of my life. I had experienced God's grace for my salvation, but I had not encountered His grace like this. I wanted to live by grace. I would have told you I was a "grace" person. I loved grace for me, but often I held others accountable to the law and all its demands. I kept asking myself this question, "How does grace work when you are hurting and broken?" There were many lessons still yet to be learned but this was the beginning of my new freedom in Christ. I wanted grace to win.

I placed that plaque on the edge of our kitchen counter for Mark to see when he came home from work. It was a stretch for me. I remember Mark walking in from work still dealing with his own shame and guilt. He walked towards me with the weight of the previous truth of betrayal and pornography. We wore our emotions like a torn piece of clothing. We were exposed and raw. I met him at the edge of the kitchen counter where the plaque sat. After months and months of counseling, I believe this was our turning point in our marriage. Mark picked up the plaque and read it. We both began to cry. I think this was the first time in months I allowed him to just touch me. We hugged and cried together.

I could not have perfectly scripted this moment if I tried. I had worship music playing when Mark walked in. Worship music playing in the house was not unusual.

It helped me survive during this time. David Crowder's recording of "How He Loves Us" just happened to be playing. And the lyrics to the song, "I don't have time to maintain these regrets when I think about… the way He loves us Oh, how He loves us" came blasting through our speakers. Jesus loved me, and Jesus loved Mark. I have to say, I felt God's delight in our hug. I even believe maybe The Father was hugging us, holding us together during the most difficult season of our marriage and life. We still had mountains to climb, but Christ was with us.

That plaque with the scripture became the foundation for rebuilding our marriage. It hangs in our office at home. I stare at it constantly. God's Word was living and offering us a new life.

"If I speak in the tongues of men and of angels, but have not love, I am a noisy gong or a clanging cymbal. And if I have prophetic powers, and understand all mysteries and all knowledge, and if I have all faith, so as to remove mountains, but have not love, I am nothing. If I give away all I have, and if I deliver up my body to be burned, but have not love, I gain nothing."

"Love is patient and kind; love does not envy or boast; it is not arrogant or rude. It does not insist on its own way; it is not irritable or resentful; it does not rejoice at wrongdoing, but rejoices with the truth. Love bears all things, believes all things; hopes all things, endures all things.

Love never fails."
I Corinthians 13: 1-7 (ESV)

I remembered studying scripture about God and His love when I ran across I John 4:7-8 (ESV). I think it goes perfectly with the 1 Corinthians 13 passage.

"Beloved, let us love one another, for love is of God; and everyone who loves is born of God and knows God. He who does not love does not know God, for God is love."

This was another eye-opening moment for me. God's Word began to speak to my heart, "If I am love, (and God is) I want you to take my name 'GOD' and put it in the passage of 1 Corinthians."

I read the passage again, and this time it read, "God" bears all things, "God" believes all things, "God" hopes all things, "God" endures all things, and "God" never fails.

I felt so much healing in seeing and knowing God never fails. The Word continued to heal my wounded heart.

God did what my human efforts could not do. I could not bear all things, but God could. I could not believe all things, but God did. I certainly could not hope and endure all things and clearly my love seemed to fail, but God's love for us never will fail us no matter what circumstance we find ourselves in.

I believe God can speak those same words to you that He did to me that day. He will not fail you. His reputation is flawless. He spoke those words to many who have gone before us in the Bible: Joshua, Ruth, Job, Esther. We are now called a living epistle like Paul spoke about in the New Testament. We are His next "letters" to the church. What does your letter read? I ask myself that question daily.

As I walked through those days of hardship, and as I clung to God in the midst of the battle, I realized the fight belonged to him. I did not know what Mark wanted for the future, but I knew what I wanted. I wanted to join the fight for what God promised me. I did not want our children to suffer through what I had suffered through as a young child. I was driven by my commitment to protect my children and our marriage. I knew what kind of man Mark had always been. As we healed, God brought a new perspective to us.

It was a season when our relationship was tested. Where emotional wounds needed to be healed, and a place where God was teaching us both lessons and giving us valuable tools. I trusted God for a result that was far off.

The result of choosing to stay and fight for our marriage has shown plentiful goodness. We survived the season in Tampa, Florida, and decided the best place for our hearts to mend and rest was at home. With much prayer, we moved our family back home to Georgia to begin again.

As sure as we pursued rest, God pursued us with His presence. As I mentioned earlier, God brought us home and planted us in a church to heal. We did not minister at this place. We sat in a sea of others and I am sure no one knew our names for a while. I was very reluctant to even go to church at first, because I didn't trust the church leadership. But as I sought after more and more healing, God began to answer my heart about my true identity. I read many books during this time. I was hungry for wisdom to navigate our rebuilding. But this is when our marriage and our journey became personal. Who was I?

Mark and I went anonymously one night to a prayer service. No one knew us as pastors. We received prayer from a complete stranger. I remember being told that evening in prayer, "God was cutting the puppet strings from old ways of doing things in ministry. Ministry would look different from the way we previously had done ministry from this day forward." I thought, who told you we were in ministry? He recommended we read books about sonship. Specifically, one book called *Spiritual Slavery to Sonship* by Jack Frost. According to this book, I was indeed living a "slavery mentality" with an orphan's heart. I needed to come home to my Father's love.

"Sonship is a heart that feels at rest and secure in God's love; it believes it belongs. It is free from shame and self-condemnation. It walks in honor toward all people, and it is willing to humble itself before man and God. It is subject to God's mission to experience His love and to give it away." Jack Frost

The spiritual slavery mentality agreed with my habits, and all the brokenness in my life and past wounds. My heart felt orphaned with no place to really trust someone's love. This book was giving words to how I felt. I had not fully trusted anyone, including God, with my wounded heart. He was a Father waiting on my return to His love and His freedom. I had been enslaved to my own wrong thinking, and Jesus was coming to my rescue.

He saw me far off, like the prodigal son, and He ran to me. He ran to my heart. He met me with His embrace. I didn't even know what an orphan's heart or a slavery mentality looked liked. But God was bringing me to the rightful place of a son, as a daughter of Christ. My thirst only gave way to another drink of the Living Water.

"But there is no need to be ashamed of tears, for tears

bore witness that a man had the greatest of courage, the courage to suffer." Viktor Frankl, *Man's Search for Meaning*.

I had a choice. You have a choice. God's reformation is not easy. Old thought patterns and wrong ways of believing were unsettling to me. Who was I now? It was another mini death I experienced, laying to rest the old me. Grieving is not for the faint of heart, but unless we embrace grief and let it have its full expression, how can we be resurrected?

Dear Jesus,

I am aware that pain, unmet needs, and trauma are a part of our lives. Some days are just hard. We live in a broken world in need of you. I pray, Father God, for you to release your truth of who we are in you. Our purpose and identity are within us. There are no spiritual shortcuts. Forgivingness opens up the door to the miraculous. I believe now you are releasing how much you love us and just how valuable we are to you, to our family, to our spouse, and most importantly, to ourselves. Let us see just how amazing your grace really is for our lives. Help us let people who hurt us off the hook. We desperately need you and your grace. Love us to our deepest needs. Walk us through the stages of grief to discover who we really are in you. When we are stripped away, reform us.

In Jesus Name,

Amen

Ask yourself, "What lies am I believing?" (Ask God if you are believing a lie......pause here and listen.) What is it?

_____

_____

_____

_____

Then repent for agreeing with that lie. Spend time journaling or praying.

_____

_____

_____

_____

_____

Then ask God, "What does your truth say about me now?" (Please write it down.)

_____

_____

_____

_____

_____

THE BEAUTIFUL UGLY TRUTH

chapter six
Identity and Legacy

Identity is defined as "who someone is; the distinguishing character or personality of an individual."

<u>There is no time frame for finding yourself after a betrayal. Healing takes some time.</u> Rediscovering myself took me on a journey. There are no set rules when grieving a loss. Though I had not suffered a divorce or a death, I lost a part of what our marriage looked like for seventeen years. When I felt I took one step forward in the process and three steps back, I was grieving. When I was angry one minute and loved him the next, I was grieving. When I wanted to dive into all his text messages and emails one minute and throw his computer away the next, I was grieving. **Grief is the cost of loving someone. And love is worth it.**

David Kessler, grief expert and author of *Finding Meaning: The Sixth Stage of Grief*, stated,

"You don't have to experience grief, but you can only avoid it by avoiding love. Love and grief are inextricably intertwined."

If you are grieving deeply, it only means you loved deeply. It is not bad to love deeply. It can only be harmful when we choose not to grieve fully. I was scared of grief, honestly. I was afraid if I allowed what I was really feeling to surface, I would get stuck in one of the other stages. I did not want to deny what we walked through, but I didn't want to remain angry anymore. I didn't want to be broken and sad either, but I could not accept where we found ourselves. We were different. But being different can be a good thing. I have since discovered you only get stuck in grief when you decide it's too painful of a process, and you shut down your ability to walk through each stage. It is human nature to not want to feel the pain associated with the loss. But in doing so we cut off our emotions. That is not a healthy way to process your feelings. I have heard our emotions are like wavelengths, music notes of sorts, and that they must travel. If we do not let the emotions and pain of grief travel through us, we can potentially get stuck. David Kessler said in an article, "Emotions need motions."

During a grieving season I encourage you to be kind to yourself. Do not rush the process. There is a glorious season on the other side, but you must experience it. Yes, Mark and I were working our way through trying to save our marriage, but there was a loss. So, what was beyond grief? I asked myself who was I?

Knowing I was created in God's image, and there would be meaning to this grief, I set out on an incredible new journey of self-discovery with me and God.

> *"God created man in His own image."*
> *Genesis 1:27 (ESV)*

Mark and I were made one when we made the covenant of marriage before God, our family, and friends. And during the crushing season of our marriage, I often thought, how was I so deceived? How was Mark deceived? I knew God had more for me than anger, hurt, and resentment from this past season. I desperately wanted to be free from this pain. I wanted to walk as the confident woman God created me to be. My hope was to feel normal again. After months of counseling, I gave myself permission to find significance in my search.

My heart felt orphaned on so many levels. My parents got a divorce, my personal struggles that surfaced in my own marriage, and desperately jumping through hoop after hoop to gain acceptance and love from others left me emotionally exhausted. It wasn't until I was at my own personal place of brokenness that I became a real seeker of who God was to me. As I studied about God and His character, it wasn't long before I realized I needed my idea of who God was to me to be healed. I remember in my anger one day (anger is a part of grief and healing), I felt His voice inside of me say, "You believe I am like your earthly father, and you don't believe I am good."

I sat on that thought for a minute. I accepted Jesus as my Savior and the Holy Spirit as my teacher and comforter, but did I accept God as a good Father who was accepting, supportive, responsible, and providing?

God to me was a picture of my earthly father, and both of those relationships needed more healing. I loved my dad, I really did. And I knew my dad loved me, but I constantly fought for his acceptance, his support, and his provision and purpose. <u>Remember if we do not find these four core basic needs from God</u> we will be left seeking them from others. I did not receive those things as a young child growing up, and God wanted to transform my concept of what a good Father is like. I didn't believe God or my dad were accepting, supportive, responsible, and would provide for me. My identity was skewed, because what I thought about God was not true.

A.W. Tozer penned in *The Knowledge of The Holy*,

"What comes into our minds when we think about God is the most important thing about you."

"The reason why many are still troubled, still seeking, still making little forward progress is because they haven't yet come to the end of themselves. We're still trying to give orders and interfering with God's work within us."

What we think about God is the most important thing about you. It's true.

I am a co-heir with Christ (Romans 8:17), which means I am a daughter of God. And I was in the middle of the wrestle. My new perspective didn't take place overnight. It was a process, but soon my orphaned, broken heart had to find a home in Father God.

The more I learned about God as my Father, the more Christ walked me through the painful process of betrayal, and I began finding myself again on the other side.

The more we understand the Nature of God and who He truly is, the more healing becomes possible in other relationships.

Mark and I committed to repair what had been broken, but the search had to come from within. I kept asking Mark for more truth, the whole truth. But when God began to change me, I no longer believed we were in a court of law. We both had work to do. This was not about who was right or wrong anymore; it was about finding grace for each other. It was about discovering the truth, just like I had asked. However, the truth I asked from Mark was not the truth I needed or the truth that would heal me.

The truth I discovered was my truth about who I was in God. And what my place was in this world.

Emotions and Events

When God held my most fragile heart like a glass ornament, He began to walk me through stages of emotional healing to set me free. I discovered some of my most painful, emotional events were inflicted on me when I was young. Yes, we were in a broken stage of our marriage, but the pain of my parent's divorce lay at my heart's door, telling me lies that we would be next to walk this path. Healing these places of trauma was the key to healing my marriage. I began to study how we typically attach an emotion to an event. Emotional events remain in our brain unless we are willing to walk back in order to walk forward. Left unhealed, we develop triggers in our emotions, and we wait for someone to touch the land mine of unresolved pain to complicate our current situation.

Forgiveness was the beginning of the healing process. I believe because I was open to forgiving, it allowed God to go deeper in the areas of healing for me. Remember, forgiveness sets you free. It was during my quiet times in this season when God began to bring up memories in my past that He wanted to heal. Personal memories of pain when I was younger. Memory by memory, with my eyes closed, He would ask me where He was during the painful event. Each time, I sensed His presence protecting me. It changed the way I viewed these events as a young child that caused so much pain in my memories. Unknowingly, I carried those painful memories into my present circumstances because I had linked an emotion to an event. Forgiveness, accepting grace, and letting God reform my thoughts put me on a new path. The Father healed me and set me free to move forward without baggage from my past. Mark and I still had work to accomplish and trust to rebuild, but knowing God had gone before us made our path a little more straight.

Rebuilding Trust

I have couples ask us all the time, "How did you rebuild trust?" The most important thing that helped me was understanding forgiveness and trust are two different things. I could offer forgiveness because I decided it was the right thing to do, but trusting Mark again would take some time. It was one day at a time, one decision at a time, and one act of rebuilding the trust at a time.

After months of counseling, Mark did something which aided in the healing process. With the guidance of our counselor, He began to own his part of how our marriage got to this place. He owned every painful decision he had made. One by one, he would ask me to forgive him. He validated my feelings and my heart with his remorse. He had allowed boundaries to be crossed and the virtual world into our home. He often spoke of feelings of shame afterwards, but the pull of the virtual force was stronger some days than he could fight. If we were going to partner with God to heal our marriage, we would need to rebuild trust in one another. As we began the process of reconciling, I fought just as hard for my new identity in my Father God.

Mark had to come clean. And I needed to know he had nothing to hide. God's grace met us at every turn. I was willing to give him the safe place to open up, and he was willing to not lie about his struggles and short-comings anymore. In all of this, I discovered who I was, and more importantly, that Mark was only human.

God was not human. Mark was God's son. And I was God's daughter. Christ gave us the power to overcome and the strength to do so. I learned we must go to the source that offers strength to us. He will give you the strength to endure.

There were days I asked about details of Mark's deception. I soon learned I did not need every detail. Even our counselor said every detail would be impossible for him to relay. I knew what I needed to know and "every detail" was not going to make things better. However, in his effort to move forward, Mark offered his phone, his contacts, his computer, all his passwords, and anything else I needed.

It showed me his willingness to embrace the process. He got used to my calls about where he was or when he was coming home. Mark was willing to be an open book for the sake of our marriage. I'm sure there were days when he was tired of the calls or texts while he was at the grocery store, but he didn't show it. He offered his phone or his computer anytime for a history check. He said he began to see the pain in my eyes that he had caused. Soon into the restoration process, Mark termed the phrase for me "space and grace." When the questions from me became frequent, he would look at me and tell me, "You have nothing but space and grace from me."

Acknowledging the hurt he caused was a big part of our rebuilding trust. The spouse who caused the breach of trust must be willing to become an open book. They must be willing to answer all of your questions as trust is being restored. Seeking Godly mental health counseling was a beneficial part of our healing process also. My part included forgiveness and seeking who I was again, not just as Mark's wife, not as a pastor's wife, not as the boys' mother, not as an Interior Designer, but as a daughter of God. Sadly, the title, daughter, was the one I was least associated with, but my concept of that was changing.

Accountability was another piece in rebuilding trust. Mark was willing to be accountable, not just to me, but to our counselor and Godly friends. I believe the spouse needs all kinds of different accountability. Yes, we are part of the accountability, but not all of it. I was patient with Mark and he was very patient with me during this time. God gave us both grace for each day. I am sure there were days when Mark wished I would just get over it, but even today, several years later, he still looks into my eyes and offers anything I need to settle my heart. "Space and Grace," he said. "I created this and I will give you all the space and grace to walk it out with me." **I had to release my fears to God and my forgiveness to Mark.**

Our counselor encouraged us both along the way. She encouraged Mark for being open and honest with me and she encouraged me for being willing to walk in forgiveness. The insecurities during this time were not as constant as it once was.

However, during one of many wrestling matches I had with my feelings one day, I reached out to Dr. Sandy. I called her, and we discussed how I didn't want to keep asking questions or having feelings of fear with Mark. She reminded me how far we had come and to continue the path of rebuilding trust and forgiveness each day. She also reminded Mark when I asked him if he was "okay" years later, that the question really meant, "How are you doing, Mark?" "Are you struggling with the tendency to go online?" She encouraged Mark not to get frustrated. She said to Mark he put those questions on "the list" and eventually, as time continued to heal us, those questions would eventually drop off my list.

One of my favorite quotes is in the book *I Surrender All* by Clay and Renee Cross. She penned these words that I hold dearly in my heart. She said this about her own husband, Clay: "Releasing the past is easier said than done but rebuilding trust demands it." (pg102)

I have discovered along the way **my greatest pain became my biggest blessing**. It has brought Mark and me back to a more intimate place. I needed to learn who God was as my Father, and base my life on that truth. I was still me, but God was empowering me to be a reflection of who He was. My greatest need was to know God and be known by Him in order for trust to be rebuilt. Trusting in God first was a must. Rebuilding trust in Mark and our marriage was going to take time. A friend told me, "until you can trust Mark, trust God in Mark."

I am so thankful God brought us back home to Georgia to heal. Though I was relying on God and trusting Him, I still had trust issues not only with Mark, but with the church. My weakness was I did not feel protected. Even after we returned home, it would be weeks before we would even consider going to a church. I still loved God, but I had gaping issues about going to a church. I wasn't sure if I could open up my heart again. After some time, we had some close friends invite us to their church. It took some time to say yes to the invitation, but I can now say it was a huge part of our healing. My tendency was to shut down and emotionally close off. Remember we talked about it in an early chapter. Not only was our past turn of events painful to us, but for me to be open and trust members of a church was going to take some more time. God was healing me in layers. I wanted to be known in this next season, but it would mean I needed to be known. I needed to open my heart up to love again.

One of my girlfriends invited me to the Thursday morning women's prayer meeting at this church. It's documented in one of my journals. The day was June 17th. I agreed to go, but knew I did not have anything to offer the prayer meeting except my pain. I was hoping no one could see the pain even though I desperately desired for someone to relate. Would anyone notice I was a broken-hearted wife, much less a broken hearted pastor's wife? Have you ever felt two different feelings at the same time? I wanted to offer the facade that I was okay, yet I wanted help for the pain.

My friend and I arrived and walked into the room. I met some of the most beautiful treasures of God that day. The ladies were all different ages and in different stages of life. Susan, who is fun-loving, and an author. Margaret, who called Ginger and I "the GG's," is full of life and joy. Bitty, who is the most loving beautiful mother you can picture and gives amazing momma hugs. Renee, who walked in the authority of God. Cathy, who is a worship leader and was healing herself. These were just a few of the ladies I met that day.

I was greeted with all kinds of warm welcomes, and soon our prayer meeting began. One lady after another shared. We worshiped, and then someone else would share. During our time, there was a call to action. I did not want to participate. A lady began to explain about doing cardboard testimonies. We did those as youth pastors in our youth groups. You would take a piece of cardboard and write your brokenness on one side and on the other side of the cardboard, write a word of how God redeemed your brokenness. The testimony part of it was an individual would stand up without saying a word and share one side of her cardboard and then flip it over for others to read. Cue the worship music and start the parade. I knew quickly I was out. I did not want to participate but the group was too small for me to hide.

Even though there was plenty in the past, God had done, this was a new season for me and the rest of our healing story had not yet been written. I acted like the good participating pastor's wife. I did manage to write the word "depleted" on one side of the card, but had nothing for the other side. I listened as one lady after another shared their pain and their victories. Faith did arise in my heart, but not enough to share my journey. I remember one sweet, older lady named Sheri came and sat beside me. She put her hand on my shoulder and leaned over and whispered in my ear, "O dear, why is your heart so heavy?" It didn't take much for me to begin crying. She continued to speak words of trust and faith in Christ into me. And then she assured me this season was a season of rest for Mark and me. And left me with this, "You think God has brought you here to sit you down, and I tell you, He has brought you here to raise you up. This season of rest is really a promotion for you." I cried more during the prayer meeting and on the way home. I had agreed to come back the following week.

Soon, Mark and I decided to attend on Sundays. We laugh now about the path we beat into the carpet after each Sunday service having someone pray for us at the altar. It's incredible how the messages preached were just what we needed to hear. And the prayer time afterward was just what we needed in order to heal. I can honestly say, the body of Christ is where deep healing can happen. God intended for us to be together and to need one another. I am not going to lie, it took me a while to trust the leadership and the pastoral staff. Often, I had to remind myself, they are human, just like my husband and just like me. None of us are perfect and neither is the church. But we are not meant to be alone. We need each other. This body loved us and was committed to showing the love of Christ to us. With time, we finally shared our raw story with the pastors and their spouses. Oh, how they have loved us well. When we shared our story, they even shared parts of their brokenness to increase our faith. Nothing is over until God says it's over. My friend, if you are still drawing breath, God is not finished. Far from it. He still has a plan for you.

> *"For I know the plans I have for you,*
> *declares the Lord, plans for welfare and not*
> *for evil, to give you a future and a hope."*
> *Jeremiah 29:11 (ESV)*

You have not wandered too far. There is no hurt God cannot heal. He is the Master. God has a plan He desires to reveal to us. This scripture is so powerful. This passage still speaks. The prophet Jeremiah was prophesying this passage to God's chosen people while spending years in exile.

Exile is the state of being barred from one's native country, typically for political or punitive reasons. I definitely felt in exile. Our rhythm was off. I was used to one way of living and believing.

Identity and Legacy

There have been more nuggets along the way to our reformation. This particular one came from a book I was reading called *Becoming Myself: Embracing God's Dream of You* by Stasi Eldredge. I highly recommend any of the Eldredges' books, John or Stasi. I love *Waking the Dead* by John Eldridge. They have both been a part of our reformation journey. But in Stasi's book, I read the chapter called "Beauty Forged by Suffering." It is a quote too good not to repeat. She had talked about a dear friend of hers whose son received his heavenly reward, way too early in her opinion, with the courageous fight against cancer. Days before he died, his grieving mother wrote this: "Father Richard has helped me to understand **if we don't let pain transform us, we will surely transmit it.**" (page 175). I need to say it again.

If we don't let pain transform us, we will surely transmit it.

Dear friend, let all the pain in your life transform you. Jesus offers beauty from our ashes.

> *"The Spirit of the Lord is upon Me,*
> *Because the Lord has anointed Me.*
> *To bring good news to the poor;*
> *He has sent Me to bind up the brokenhearted.*
> *To proclaim liberty to the captives,*

And the opening of the prison to those who are bound;
To proclaim the year of the Lord's favor,
And the day of vengeance of our God.
To comfort all who mourn,
To grant to those who mourn in Zion,
To give them a beautiful headdress instead of ashes,
The oil of gladness instead of mourning,
The garment of praise instead of a faint spirit;;
That they may be called oaks of righteousness,
The planting of the Lord, that He may be glorified.
They shall build up the ancient ruins;
they shall raise up the former devastations;
they shall repair the ruined cities,
the devastations of many generations."
Isaiah 61:1-4 (ESV)

Our identity is forged like gold. Even though the bad stuff or painful events have to rise to the top, what remains when we are in the fire is worth it. I believe our transformation and identity are not only for us and our refreshing, but also for our children and our children's children. **Our identity is connected to our legacy. The greatest gift we want to leave our children is a legacy.** Legacy only progresses in the coming generations. Our story, this book, is not just about Mark and me. It is realizing we are not just living and contending for ourselves and our well-being, but for our children and our children's children and their health and well-being. For you and your children. We can transmit our identity anew, our true identity to our children or we can transmit a warped version of God and our pain to our children. It's our choice.

I know life circumstances are not easy. It was not easy in the middle of my pain. Some days I wanted a quick way of escape, but what reward would that leave our children? Please know, I understand there are some circumstances and brokenness in relationships that you must leave for you and your children's long term health. There is no condemnation here. Marriages are not perfect. Raising children is not perfect. I understand choices are made for us sometimes. But if you have the choice, I pray God heals your heart and your marriage. Especially, let God heal what you believe about Him.

If your marriage does not heal, let God heal your heart. Your identity affects your legacy. God's love is relentless towards you. Remember, after a season of grief, you will walk through a season of rediscovery.

Discovering who I was in light of all of this upheaval was a journey I needed to take. I really wanted to know. I had prayed in many of my prayers for God to show me my identity. As a young pastor's wife, I learned early on I could not give away what I did not have. What was I missing? I had studied and taught for some time about being the bride of Christ. I believed I was a new creation and old things had passed away (2 Corinthians 5:17), but experiencing sonship (daughter-ship) was uncharted territory. I began to study more about what sonship meant. Sonship is being fully loved and fully accepted. Exposing my orphan's heart during this time meant more healing for me. God was my Father, and I was His child. He loved me. I did not have to earn His love. I learned sonship is not enjoyed by natural birth, but must be received through adoption. God was taking me deeper into my relationship with Him and into my new identity. I belonged. I was adopted. I was being reformed. And so are you.

Dear Jesus,

I proclaim our full identity. Set us free in our old thought patterns and walk us into our inheritance. Thank you that we can walk in all you have proclaimed in your Word. Healing for our broken heart, liberty to what holds us captives, the opening of prison doors, the acceptable year of the Lord, to comfort all who mourn, your beauty for our ashes and the oil of joy and the garment of praise for the spirit of heaviness. We will be called trees of righteousness, and in all this, you will be glorified. Glorify your name through us. Deliver us and cause yourself to shine through us. My identity is in you. Heal us to teach generations about the goodness of who you really are, a good Father.

In the beautiful name of Jesus,
Amen

What perception of God needs to be healed in you?

_____

_____

_____

_____

_____

_____

_____

What emotional events would you like God to heal in you? Tell Him about it.

_____

_____

_____

_____

_____

_____

_____

_____

THE BEAUTIFUL UGLY TRUTH

chapter seven
Our Rightful Place

My perception of God was being healed. I truly began to feel the upheaval season of our marriage was for my good. I was beginning to trust God as a good Father. My past wounds were only allowed to forge a new understanding of what God's character truly was, and who He created me to be. My transformation did not happen overnight.

The OT scholar, Walter Brueggemann, has developed a helpful way to categorize the Psalms and bring them into our personal journey. The process of transformation begins with Orientation, Dis-orientation, and Re-orientation. I can honestly say up to this point, I was only familiar with orientation and disorientation. Re-orientation is the place where we realize God has brought us through a dis-orientative state and we are in a new place of gratitude and awareness. My transformation process took time. Just like grieving takes time.

I remember a particular afternoon in November, soon after we arrived back home to Georgia, when encouragement came my way. I thought I was just going over to a friend's house who was hosting an open house for her hand-made jewelry. Sometimes, God interrupts your day with a little extra encouragement from Himself. Another one of my dear friends, Amanda, whom I had not gotten to see since I had been back in Atlanta, was there. I didn't want to load her down with all the details for our return. It was just great to see some familiar faces. I remember as we were both standing in the living room catching up, she spoke of this book I am writing today. "Write the book," she said to me. "God is saying, write the book." God would turn this season around. I had no idea this book would be part of my re-orientation, but Father God did.

Years later, here it is. I was so encouraged by our meeting, but writing a book seemed too far off in the distance. I mean, honestly, the emotions of our return and life back in Georgia were too raw at the time. I am sure these confessions of a pastor's wife would have been full of some very colorful language years ago. It may not have made it to print. It was encouraging to think God could get glory out of this process. We hugged, and I continued to shop. I ended up purchasing a necklace. It was copper in color with a rectangular-shaped pendant.

The word scripted on it was "BE." It spoke to me during this season. I felt the Father's approval for me to just BE. I did not need to do anything or be anything for anybody. Even being a wife with two very active boys, my heart was embracing the idea of this small word.

Later the same evening, another friend I had not seen since we had left Florida was there. This couple had prayed and ministered to Mark and me years prior. Their names are Ed and Karen. After I had purchased my goods, Karen asked if she could pray for me before we left. I love how God showed her how desperate my heart was in the moment. We all sat down. Karen and Ed sat to my left, Ginger was in front of me, and Amanda sat on my right side. Karen and Ed began to pray for me. I am still waiting for some of the things they prayed over me to come to pass, but one thing they prayed pierced my heart.

Karen said, "God would destroy a ministry to save a relationship." All I could think was how did she know? Mark and I had just recently returned to Georgia, still very broken with no ministry opportunities in sight. I was literally watching part of her prayer unfold. God did destroy a "ministry" to save a relationship. It was going to be months later before I truly began to understand the true meaning of what God was trying to say to me. I believe now God was leading me to re-orientation.

For me, the rightful place and re-orientation were

about engaging with God as my Father. I was His daughter with no strings attached. I lived most of my Christian walk as a servant for Him with an orphan's heart. Though it was noble, God desires a deeper relationship with His family. I was happy most of the time to give and to serve. However, God was not interested in leaving me in this condition of false humility or false identity. He had "greater" for me, and He has "greater" for anyone else who struggles with this concept of serving for approval. Please do not misunderstand me here. I unintentionally lived with my servanthood mentality. I thought I was doing the right thing. I have desired most of my life for the attention of my earthly father and my heavenly Father. Nevermind, I already had both of their attention. I thought I had to behave good enough, do all the right things for God, and serve Him out of obligation in order to obtain His love and favor. Basically, I learned how to live by rules, trust in my own acts of service, and was confident if all else failed, my tithe was the ticket into God's love and favor. The law made sense in my mind even though I felt it was impossible to live up to its requirements until I had my children. The Ten Commandments to me was a list of rules I thought I could not follow. After I had children, I realized the law was part of God's grace also. They were a guidepost to keep me moving forward in my life. The law actually pointed me to Jesus and his better covenant.

I learned I did not have to work, and work, and work. Just like the Prodigal Son's older brother looking for his father's love and approval. The sad thing about this story is, not only did the oldest son already have his father's approval, but he had his inheritance too. All the father's inheritance was his, yet the older son's orphan heart was exposed by the father's extravagant love.

"And he said to him, 'Your brother has come, and
your father has killed the fattened calf, because he
has received him back safe and sound.'
But he was angry and refused to go in.
His father came out and entreated him,
But he answered his father, 'Look! These many
years I have served you, and I never disobeyed
your command. You never gave me a young goat
that I might celebrate with my friends.
But when this son of yours came, who has
devoured your property with prostitutes,
you killed the fattened calf for him!'
And he said to him, 'Son, you are always with
me, and all that is mine is yours.
It was fitting to celebrate and be glad,
for this your brother was dead and is alive!
He was lost and is found!"
Luke 15:27-32 (ESV)

My heart felt exposed when I read this passage. I thought I had done everything right to find favor with God in my life. Yet discovering this place felt uncomfortable to me. I wanted to be healed and whole. This was the true longing in my heart. But honestly, I just wanted someone to run after me. This was one of the hardest places I found myself in. I sadly related to the older brother in this story. I was busy trying to be right and honestly felt in this moment God was unfair. Thank goodness God was teaching me He was fair. None of us are perfect on this side of heaven. It was while looking in the mirror of this passage, that I envisioned Father God running all the way back to the first place my heart felt orphaned. All the way back to the living room when I was nine. He met me through all my emotional traumas growing up. He scooped me up and wrapped me up in His wings. I finally found my resting place in God. He no longer wanted my heart to feel orphaned. He had an inheritance of His extravagant love for me to encounter. All that belongs to the Father, is mine. And all that belongs to the Father, is yours.

The Holy Spirit was my teacher. I spent waking mornings and endless nights with Him. I worked and took care of my family, but any chance I got to sit quietly with God, I went after it. It was then He began to speak to me about stepping into my transformation.

Sonship is about having the heart of the Father. Jesus was sent to earth as a son. His life is our best example. He honored his Father, and only did what his Father told him. It was my identity. I was a daughter. I soon learned if I wanted to be a mother, physically or spiritually, I had to be a daughter first. I needed to submit, honor, and love. God was busy replenishing my depleted heart and making it whole again.

I began to read more about sonship and honor. I was growing in God's love and studying His Word fervently. One particular day, I was sitting at my desk. It was a picturesque day outside. I remember the sun shining through my front bay window of our family home. I had the day off of work and decided to stay home and sit with my Father. The boys were still at school, so it was nice and quiet. It was at this moment while sitting at my desk I heard God whisper to my heart, "Now I want to share my glory with you, Gwen."

I sat quietly, stunned. I am not sure how long I sat in that moment before my heart replied, "You can't do that!"

I remember my thoughts racing back and forth. I honestly felt like I was having a conversation with someone. I knew this voice was my Teacher. I would not have thought of saying this by myself. I remember thinking of the passage in Isaiah that God doesn't share his glory. But why was my Father telling me something else?

"I am the Lord; that is My name; my glory I give to
no other, nor My praise to carved idols. Behold, the
former things have come to pass, and new things I now
declare; before they spring forth I tell you of them."
Isaiah 42:8-9 (ESV)

I felt my Father's voice speaking to me. I believed it wholeheartedly, but I thought if I told anyone, they would string me up by my heels and call me a heretic. Why was this concept foreign to me? I was even careful to speak about it with Mark until I continued to do more studying. However, at one point I remember asking Mark if God really could share His glory with man. Does He want to share it with all His sons and daughters? Maybe that is what He meant when He said He would come after a bride without spot or blemish. I often thought, how would we be able to be without spot or blemish on this side of heaven. Only with His righteousness, His glory, and fully knowing who we are in Him. We buried our heads into the book of Isaiah, and discovered that Isaiah was speaking about the coming of the Christ in the context of Isaiah 42:8-9.

"I am the Lord; that is My name! And My glory I will not give <u>to another</u>," (emphasis added). The word "another" stood out to me. I love how God declared His name at the very beginning of this verse. In some translations of the scriptures, it says, "I am the Lord, Jehovah, that is my name!"

Matthew Henry said regarding Isaiah 42:8, "Jehovah is the name he made himself known by when He began to perform promises to the patriarchs. It is He, the Lord, that gives birth to all things and the promises of His word breathed over us and in us. And NOT giving His glory <u>to another</u> meant anyone or any image that stood in competition with Him."

How could anybody or any other deity compete with a resurrected King? To drive this point home in my heart, Mark found the Strong's Concordance defined the word '<u>another</u>' in Hebrew as 'stranger.' Therefore, in implication, God is saying His glory will not be given to a stranger or another deity. But He has given His glory to Christ, His son. They are one. And just as they are one, we also are one when we accept Christ as our Savior. He then lives inside of us and we become the righteousness of God through Christ.

Even with this understanding of Isaiah and what God was revealing to me, my heart was longing for more. I was quick to ask God to show me this truth of "sharing His glory" in the new covenant. Christ was our new covenant; a better covenant. My next thought as I prayed was, "Check out John 17."

I love John 17. It's one of my favorite chapters in the

whole bible. Years prior, God brought me to this chapter when He began to reveal His love for me. This chapter in John is about a conversation Jesus had with His Father before He went to the cross. I often thought I would have loved to be a fly on the wall listening to the conversation between God and His son so many years ago. Okay, maybe not a fly. I sat with this conversation in my mind. I closed my eyes and a picture in my imagination began to unfold. Christ is praying to Father God before He dies a cruel death by crucifixion. He is talking to his Father about himself, about his disciples, about his church, and about us. He would be betrayed by Judas soon. Maybe betrayal was a prerequisite to glory. Christ tells the rest of His disciples at dinner about His soon departure. Christ announces to Peter of his denial. Jesus answers Thomas's questions about how we will know the way to him. He said, "I am the way, the truth, and the life." Jesus goes on to answer Phillip's question of seeing the Father. Christ replies, "If you have seen me, you have seen my Father." I often believe Jesus was actually speaking to all of us through these questions and reminds us that we just need to stay connected to Him. He is the Vine. We are connected. He commands us to love one another and promises us the Holy Spirit, our new teacher. And then Jesus has this one-on-one conversation with His Father on our behalf.

"I made known to them your name, and I will
continue to make it known, that the love with which
you have loved me may be in them, and I in them."
John 17:26 (ESV)

I remembered years ago when God brought His love to me through this particular scripture and the reading of His Word. I would sit and meditate on this passage for hours, "that the love with which you loved Me (Jesus) may be in them."

I desire to be completely, perfectly loved. Sadly, for many years I desired this love from other broken vessels. Without Jesus, we are all a little broken. It's not bad to desire love, but Christ came to love us so we could love ourselves and others. **Love like Jesus loves.** Well, there is a new wristband!

Like I mentioned, I camped out in John 17 for many years. I read the passages, listened to worship music, prayed, and bathed myself in His perfect love for me. Have you ever read scripture before, and saw something you've never seen before? I was wondering when God snuck this part of the scripture in John 17.

God kept nudging me to reread the chapter. The whole chapter in context. How could I miss something so important? If you have not read the chapter, I encourage you to stop and read it now. I pray it will refresh you.

So, I read it again and there it was. In bright red letters in verse twenty-two.

"And the glory that You have given Me, I have given to them, that they may be one just even as We are one."
John 17:22 (ESV)

There were those beautiful, life-changing words. For us, you and me, to become one heart and mind with Father God. It is identity in Christ, to share in the very glory of God, and called by name in His righteousness.

I ran back to Matthew Henry's commentary this time to read John 17:22.

"The glory which thou gave me, as the trustee or channel of conveyance, I have accordingly given them, to this intent, that they may be one, as we are one; so that those gifts will be in vain, IF they be not one."

God has bestowed upon us spiritual gifts, for His kingdom to come on earth. When we are one with Christ, those gifts are not in vain anymore because God has a plan and a purpose for our gifts. But it is about the gift of who Christ is in us that makes our spiritual gifting come alive. Matthew Henry goes on to say, "The glory of being in covenant with The Father, and accepting him, of being laid on his bosom and designed for a place at his right hand, was the glory which the Father gave to the Redeemer and has confirmed it to the redeemed. The honor he says he hath given them, because he hath intended it for them, setting it upon them and secured it to them upon their believing Christ's promises to be real gifts."

I was formed by my Father God. This truth was setting me free.

I struggled with my identity in Christ for years. To some degree, I believe we all do, no matter how old we are. It is by the sovereignty of God and my hunger to know Him, I found my identity. My prayer is that He will reveal it to you. I think He just wanted me to know I am His daughter and everything He has, I have. His inheritance for His children is never-ending.

I also believe He wants everyone to know their rightful place in His kingdom. We are His sons and daughters. It does not matter how we grew up or what kind of parents we had or may not have had; God wants to heal our wounds. **He wants to heal our sight so we can see ourselves the way he sees us.**

One of my life scriptures during my Christian walk has been Luke 1:45 (ESV)

> *"Blessed is she who believed, that there*
> *would be a fulfillment of those things, which*
> *were told to her from the Lord."*

I cannot tell you how many times I have prayed this scripture over myself. Lord, help me believe and then give me the courage to fulfill those things. I read this scripture over and over again. Blessed is she who believed, for there will be (present tense) a fulfillment of those things spoken to her by the Lord.

I am, and you are, a child of the King, co-heirs with Jesus. It is then we can become a "carrier of Christ." His Word and the understanding of our identity must germinate just like a baby growing in a mother's womb. And in believing, there will be a fulfillment of those things spoken to you by the Lord. I encourage you to sit for a minute in the understanding of who you are in Christ.

You are loved. You are not broken beyond repair. The world is broken, yes, but you are being made whole.

God opened my eyes when He revealed His truth in my life. The new covenant came to set us all free. How I grew up did not define me. What the doctors spoke over my body when I was sick did not terrify me anymore, and what I heard from the lips of my husband that broke my heart, did not conquer me. Walking out of this situation was like walking out of prison. The key to my padded cell just happened to be truly discovering who I was in Christ. Walking out of this mindset that once held me captive was so liberating. There are all kinds of lies the enemy tells us: you are not good enough, you will never succeed, you will always struggle with anxiety, or you will always lack. But we have a God bigger than those lies. He has called us by name and He has given us the power to overcome every lie. He has created us to share in His glory. Before we can affect the kingdom in this world, the kingdom needs to be born in our hearts to discover our position in Him. He came to set everyone who is captive free. He has come to share His glory. He shares it with His family through Jesus Christ. It is my identity in Christ. It is your identity in Christ. It is ours to share in the very glory of God, and to be called by His name.

The prophet Isaiah says it beautifully, in chapter 60,

"Arise, shine, for your light has come, and the
glory of the Lord has risen upon you."
Isaiah 60:1 (ESV)

I believe before God returns for the Bride of Christ on this earth, He will first release the sons and daughters of the King to bring about His rule and reign on this earth.

"For it is the Father's good pleasure to
give us the Kingdom."
Luke 12:32 (ESV)

The Word 'Kingdom' in Greek means His royalty, rule, and realm. "The Kingdom of God is righteousness, peace, and joy." Romans 14:17 (ESV) There is a promise God still wants to keep. We are created for Him by Him that His son would be glorified through us.

I can only be truthful with you about what He revealed to my heart. My way of seeing and hearing God may be different or foreign to some, but it is how I interact and commune with Father God I so dearly love. I pray you see Him and hear Him and desire to know Him in your own special way. And each and every trial you face will just be the stepping stones to be more like Him. I pray you are empowered to go out and change the kingdom for His glory. He prayed John 17 over you some two thousand years ago.

Mark and I have celebrated over 25 years of marriage. Jesus reigns in our family. Life has a way of putting titles on you and me. As I mentioned earlier, the one I was least associated with was the one God wanted to bring to me most, I was his daughter. Well, this cowgirl has been cow-tipping. I have been turning over every sacred cow and lie I believed about myself and to whom I belong. I hear the rhythm of the miraculous finally. It's a song with ebbs and flows, loud parts and soft ones. I love discovering the rhythm of God.

2 Corinthians 3:16-18 (ESV) instructs my heart to this,

> *"But when someone turns to the Lord, the veil is removed. For the Lord is the Spirit, and where the Spirit of the Lord is, there is freedom. So all of us, who have had that veil removed can see and reflect the glory of the Lord—who is the Spirit—makes us more and more like him as we are changed into his glorious image."*

I take great comfort in my relationship with Christ and the reading of His Word. My heart belongs to Him, and every day I am being transformed into His very image so I can glorify the Father who lives in me. I believe Him when He whispers now, "I will never fail you. I will never fail you. I will never fail you, Gwen." Because His Word says so.

> *"No man shall be able to stand before you all the days of your life. Just as I was with Moses, so I will be with you; I will not fail or forsake you. Be strong and courageous, for you shall cause this people to inherit the land that I swore to their fathers to give them."*
> *Joshua 1:5-6 (NASB)*

And my friend, God says it to you today, "I will never fail you." Ask God what your voice will contribute. Let

Hope arise. Let dreams, businesses, songs and books arise. Whatever your giftings are, may they arise to a whole new level in Christ Jesus because it will glorify Him. May His glory be spread throughout the whole earth. Be who God made you to be.

Dear Father,

Will you sit with my friend for a while?

I trust you as I reread these pages. You are transforming us to transmit you in greater measure. Let us spread your gospel with the gifting you have given us. I know sometimes we must endure hardship to find you. Give us your strength and tenacity to hold onto you firmly in order to continue.

James 1:2-5 (MSG) says.... "Consider it a sheer gift, friends, when tests and challenges come at you from all sides. You know that under pressure, your faith-life is forced into the open and shows its true colors. So don't try to get out of anything prematurely. Let it do its work so you become mature and well-developed, not deficient in any way. If you don't know what you're doing, pray to the Father. He loves to help."

In Jesus name,

Amen

What is Father God saying to you right now at this moment? Journal it here.

_____

_____

_____

_____

_____

What desire has God placed in your heart to bring Him glory?

_____

_____

_____

_____

_____

What is your next step?

_____

_____

_____

_____

_____

THE BEAUTIFUL UGLY TRUTH

chapter eight
Our Due Season

*"And let us not grow weary of
doing good, for in due season we
will reap, if we do not give up."*
Galatians 6:9 (ESV)

I am so grateful for God's Word. It teaches us how
to live life victoriously and courageously. It by no means
teaches us that hard things do not happen. Actually, quite
the opposite. It just directs us on how to be overcomers
through our faith in Christ Jesus. Being overcomers
means we "come over" particular obstacles. God has given
us the road map to do so. Including the scripture above.
Throughout scripture many examples are given to us
on how to live courageously. So, when you feel like the
world is against you, do not loosen or relax your grip on

courage. The Word of God directs our attention to live courageously, to be brave, and choose a victorious mindset.

"We have this hope as an anchor for
the soul, firm and secure."
Hebrews 6:19 (NIV)

The memories of our past trials are just that, memories. What Mark and I walked through was difficult. But it is our story. It has taken years to heal and discover our value again. Difficulties do not define who we are in a negative way. Mark is a strong man of God. He is a son in God's kingdom and I am proud to be his wife. I now know, without Christ exposing the secrets Mark held, we were powerless against the Goliaths of pornography and emotional infidelity. It is a battle we have won, but the memories are there as a testimony. We are not afraid to talk about it with others and remember it. Accountability, counseling, and even writing about it were huge parts of our healing. We pray daily for our boys against such giants. It has entered their worlds because they have mobile devices. We speak to them openly about pornography and how it destroys real intimacy in relationships and affects a normal sex life.

I also believe there are still many couples, husbands, fathers, wives, businessmen, doctors, and pastors who secretly struggle with the pulls of this mighty giant. I believe there are spouses feeling abandoned in the wake of such destruction. Maybe you are walking through this now with your spouse. Please be encouraged. It may not feel like it at the moment, but I promise God is with you and will not fail you either.

On the other hand, our story may look completely different from yours, but I promise whatever the circumstances, we can trust our seasons will change. Just like the natural seasons of life we experience, winter, spring, summer and fall, one season always gives way to another. I have studied the meaning of each season and have tried to mine the treasures of each one. If I am honest, I struggled with what could possibly be the treasure during the winter season. How could there be a treasure directly related to my 'dark night of the soul?' For me personally, the 'dark night of the soul' felt dead and everything looked dried up. I often asked myself these questions:

- Did I do something wrong?
- How did I get here?
- Where is God?

I didn't know I was in the night season of my soul until I was in the middle of what felt like the longest winter. If you are in a night season or a dark night of your soul, you are not alone. I believe it's a season we all walk through at least one time in our lives. It's a time when we transition from depending on our spouse and our own will, and become dependent on God and His will for us. It is when all the good in our life we previously depended on seems stripped away. There were areas in my life where I was completely dependent on Mark. What once felt alive and beautiful gave way to feelings of aloneness, cold, quiet, and helplessness.

During this time, and because I am such a visual learner, God began to show me things in nature through the seasons. Why did this dark night of my soul feel just like winter? I discovered during the actual season of winter when life outside can feel alone, cold, dried up, and quiet the same feelings can happen to us at our soul level. This analogy works great if you live in a place where you actually experience winter months.

Mark and I had often discussed the leaves and fruit on our trees, or the lack thereof, felt like winter to our souls and physical bodies. Leaves and fruit are what we can see on a tree that indicates life and growth. God refers to how we are known by our fruit (Matthew 7:16). Fruit and green leaves are the tangible, visible evidence of life and are the byproduct of what is at the root level. Our fruit or our leaves are only as healthy as our roots. If we want our leaves on our tree to be healthy, we must discover what is at our root level. And if we want to become the Trees of

Righteousness scripture speaks about, God may have some excavating to do in our root system.

Naturally, I began to study what happens to a tree during the cold winter months. We know it loses its beautiful leaves that provide shade, and an inability to produce fruit during winter. The tree begins to show signs it is dying a slow death. However, if the tree has a good root system, nothing could be farther from the truth. During the winter the root system's job is to grow deeper and deeper into the soil to find their nutrition and sustainability for the next season. The roots look for nutrients and water during the cold winter months underground. A tree's roots can extend into the surrounding area up to 2.5 times the tree's height.

During the dark night of my soul, I discovered I was not actually dying. The knowledge and understanding of my root system growing was a relief. To discover my roots were finding nutrition for the next season released me from trying to have it all together on the outside. It freed me from pretending the pastor and his wife were doing great. I could actually come away, rest, and look for nutrition for myself with my Father and His word. I could stop pretending to be the perfect little pastor's wife and allow God's Word to wash me, feed me, and sustain me. I am not going to lie to you, winter felt harsh. We still had many difficult days to navigate through, but my hope had changed. Winter sustained me and actually brought life back to me.

Whatever your winter season circumstances are, know that God is bringing new life back to you. This is why scripture tells us not to lose heart, grow weary, relax our courage, or faint. There is a due season for you that is full of harvest.

Mark and I have traveled through many seasons since this one. We have watched God restore many things to us: Our love, our well-being, our identity, and our finances. But this season was one of the most memorable ones.

We now have the privilege to minister to others after Jesus went to our root system and healed our own hearts. Mark shares our story often with other men, small groups, and retreats. He talks about the ways our leaves were a sign of the fruit in our root system. We encourage other couples to do the same and become emotionally healthy. Becoming emotionally healthy not only benefited us and our marriage, but it was a reward to our children and their children. When we have nothing to hide, we create intimacy. Our legacy is for our boys and we will continue to do a lot of work to stay healthy. We loved the analogy God gave us years ago about the tree, their leaves, and their root system. We have pictures of trees hanging throughout our home. They are just pictures to most, but they are memories for us of a season we survived. Every time I see one of our photographs, I am thankful for all the work God did in our lives. Because God's Word is living, He continues to unfold to us how valuable trees are to His kingdom.

> *"Blessed is the man who walks not in the counsel of the wicked, nor stands in the ways of sinners, nor sits in the seat of the scoffers; but his delight is in the law of the Lord, and on his law he meditates day and night. He is like a tree planted by streams of water that yield fruit in its season, and its leaf does not wither. In all that he does, he prospers."*
> *Psalms 1: 1-3 (ESV)*

> *"They may be called oaks of righteousness, the planting of the Lord, that he may be glorified. They shall build up the ancient ruins; they shall raise up the former devastations; they shall repair the ruined cities, the devastations of many generations."*
> *Isaiah 61:3b-4 (ESV)*

Ezekiel was one of the four major prophets in scripture along with Isaiah, Jeremiah, and Daniel. He was the first prophet to be called during the Babylonian Captivity. He was truly in exile while ministering hope to His people. His vision of dry bones in Chapter 37 was a symbol of restoration to not only Israel in her time of great need, but it continues to speak today. God has restoration for those who believe. Dry bones can come together and live again.

As I continued to study the prophet Ezekiel, I began to sense hope arising. If God could minister to the captives, He could do it again. It also gave me hope He could do it in my life.

Ezekiel 47:1-9a and 12 (ESV) states,

> *"Then he brought me back to the door of the temple, and behold, water was issuing from below the threshold of the temple towards the east (the temple faced east). The water was flowing down....*

Water signified there were signs of life again.

> *"Going on eastward with a measuring line in his hand, the man measured a thousand cubits, and then led me through the water, and it was ankle deep. Again, he measured a thousand, and led me through the water, and it was knee deep. Again, he measured a thousand, and he led me through the water, and it was waist-deep. Again, he measured a thousand and it was a river I could not pass through. And he said to me, 'Son of man, have you seen this?' Then he led me back to the bank of the river... very many trees on the one side and on the other side. And he said to me, 'This water*

flows toward the eastern region and goes down into the Arabah... and where the river goes, every living creature will come to life; and there will be many fish."

The place called Arabah in this passage actually means a "desolate and dry area." In the most dry, desolate place in your life, invite the river of God to come in. Because like scripture says, wherever the river goes, dead things will come alive again.

"And on the banks, on both sides of the river, there will grow all kinds of trees for food. Their leaves will not wither, nor their fruit fail, but they will bear fresh fruit every month, because the water for them flows from the sanctuary. Their fruit will be for food and their leaves will be for healing." (some translations says medicine)
Ezekiel 47:12 (ESV)

Have you ever felt like you were in over your head? Jesus will lead you back to the bank of the river. And wherever the river flows, life will return. Not only will life return for you, but there will be many fish. Jesus called his first disciples fishers of men and he calls us that today. And on these banks, as Ezekiel prophesied, many trees will be there. Jesus turns our winter season with our dead leaves into medicine and healing for others.

I desperately wanted to know a couple who had been through what we had been through. Now we want to be a couple that God re-orientated to help others. Letting God heal you and your spouse is one thing, giving it away is another. Secrets are not healthy for anyone; for the spouse who is secretly addicted to pornograpghy or the spouse who keeps the secret from others to protect the spouse's addiction. The power of any sin is in the secret. If you want to grow in intimacy, find others you trust and who have walked through something similar. Talk about it. We are healed when we talk about it constructively.

Recently at a marriage conference, we heard Michael Todd, a pastor out of Tulsa, OK say,

"The place of burial and the place of planting look the same in a season."

Don't mistake your planting as your burial.

"Unless a grain of wheat falls into the earth and dies,
it remains alone; but if it dies, it bears much fruit."
John 12:24 (ESV)

As you remain hidden, let the fresh water of God's Word nourish your soul. God has done a deep work in us, and continues even today. Find strength to move forward in Him.

This is my heart, to be an instrument of the rhythm

of heaven. That our condition, whatever state we find ourselves in, be strengthened in Christ Jesus to bring His rule and reign throughout the whole earth. **My identity didn't come from what I did, but rather who I belonged to.**

My identity was much more than belonging to my mom and dad, although I am grateful I carried their name. My identity was more than being a wife and now carrying my husband's last name, even though he is my love. My identity was more than being called mom, although it has been my greatest accomplishment. My whole journey thus far was about becoming just who God created me to BE.

I believe our trials push us to becoming the greatest version of ourselves and lead us to our calling. Mark and I want to be a voice to others now. We have been so blessed to mentor other couples and help them walk through the path of betrayal to healing. God has opened many doors to help others understand they are not alone.

Years ago, I sat in front of several book publishers. It was not my timing in the release of our story, but it took us to the next step. We were advised to build a website and grow our social media audience first. We did, even though we didn't have a name for the ministry yet. God was birthing something new, and out of the ground our seed was sprouting. I remember building content for our website, taking pictures, and being creative with our web designers. What would our logo be? Our name? Our mission? I was amazed at how God was moving in our lives. Reconnecting Lives Ministries was the fruit of our winter season. God changed us. We have been invited on several podcasts telling our story of reformation and restoration. And now it's time for our book to be released.

Recently, I looked up the prefix, RE. We see it in multiple words attached to a lot of ministries. RE can stand for Rebuild, Rebirth, Restore, Refresh and now Reconnecting. God wants our lives not only to be reconnected to others, but to Him. RE is a prefix with the meaning "again and again and again." It indicates repetition. What is God rebuilding in your life? What is God refreshing in your life? What is God reconnecting in your life? He will do it again and again and again.

You are worth the fight. Christ fought for you. He will not fail you. We gain territory in our lives when we begin to believe God, and what He says about us. We are His sons and His daughters. We are a carrier of His presence in the world. We do not take territory back when we try to fight the enemy, because he is already a defeated foe. We take territory back when WE BELIEVE.

Dear Jesus,

Thank you for the blessing of this journey. Thank you for who you are and that you are so aware of our circumstances. You are so alive and you have risen over us. Show us where we need your help to roll the stones away in our lives. Show us where we need to forgive and extend grace. And then I ask courageously for a due season. Our very own due season, a distinct time for a harvest in our personal lives. Let the river flow and bring life in our winter season. We know where the river flows, everything desolate and dry will come to life again. Let our fruit become nourishment to others. Let our leaves provide medicine and bring healing for others. You can do exceedingly, abundantly, above all we can ask or think. Help us believe more. Make your name known throughout the whole earth through us.

In the powerful name of Jesus Christ,
Amen

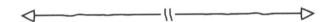

"Blessed is she who believed that there would be a fulfillment of what was spoken to her from the Lord."
Luke 1:45 (ESV)

What is God showing you again and again in your life?

_____

_____

_____

_____

_____

_____

What is God reconnecting in your life right now?
Journal here.

_____

_____

_____

_____

_____

_____

_____

Blessings on your journey, friend. May God seal the work He is doing in you until His coming. Till we meet again.

Things I Don't Want You to Forget

"My flesh and my heart may fail, but God is the *strength* of my heart and my *portion* forever."
Psalm 73:26 (ESV)

When God *speaks* things happen.

Someday everything will make *perfect* sense.

Sometimes our answers to prayers may not look or feel like God's answers, but *trusting* Him with the process is the most important thing we can do.

"For nothing is hidden except to be made manifest; nor is anything secret except to come to *light*. If anyone has ears to hear, let him hear."
Mark 4:22-23 (ESV)

"I would have lost heart unless I had believed I would see the *goodness* of the Lord in the land of the living."
Psalm 27:13 (NKJV)

God is present. I know the
storm can distract you from
His *presence* but He is there.

chapter two

Pain
leads us to
healing.

Forgiveness is
your pathway to
freedom.

Forgiveness is "for giving" our hurts,
betrayals, abandonment and all our wounds
over to the one who can heal us.

Don't fear your journey,
God has *healing* in mind.

"For if you forgive others their trespasses (their reckless and willful sins), your heavenly Father will also *forgive* you. But if you do not forgive others (nurturing your hurt and anger with the result that it interferes with your relationship with God), then your Father will not forgive your trespasses."
Matthew 6:14-15 (AMP)

chapter three

"Fear not for I am with you;
be not dismayed,
for I am your God;
I will strengthen you,
I will help you,
I will uphold you with my
righteous right hand."
Isaiah 41:10 (ESV)

If God does not remove or change whatever "it" is, He is wanting to teach, reveal and *heal* something in our lives.

"For God did not give us a spirit of timidity or cowardice or fear, but (He has given us a spirit) of power and of *love* and of *sound judgment* and *personal discipline* (abilities that result in a calm, well-balanced mind and self control)."
2 Timothy 1:7 (AMP)

Men *connect* more physically and women *connect* more emotionally.

Affirmation, security, purpose and identity are the four basic needs which come *only* from God.

"If you abide in my word, you are truly my disciples, and you will know the *truth*, and the truth will set you *free*."
John 8:32 (ESV)

Scared moments of *grace* do not feel like grace in the moment.

Without the foundation of *truth*, you have nothing to build upon.

Let God's truth of who He is and His love for you set you *free*.

Restoration
is a choice.

"God is *love.*"
I John 4:8

When we are no longer able to change a situation, we are challenged to change *ourselves.* Viktor Frankl

God's *power* is still released even in His silence or presumed absence in our lives.

The death of something is really the *birthing* of something else.

"*Love* bears all things, believes all things, hopes all things, endures all things… *Love* never fails."
I Corinthians 13:7

Grieving is not for the faint of heart, but unless we *embrace* grief and let it have its full expression, how can we be resurrected?

chapter six

Grief is the cost of loving someone.
And love is *worth* it.

If we don't let pain transform us,
we will *surely* transmit it.

Our identity is connected to our *legacy*.

Our greatest pain can become our biggest *blessings*.

Forgiveness is the beginning of the healing process.

Forgiveness and *trust* are two different things.

chapter seven

Sonship is about having the *heart* of the Father.

God will *heal* our sight so we can see ourselves the way He *sees* us.

"I am the Lord; that is My name;
my glory I give to no other, nor My
praise to carved idols. Behold, the
former things have come to pass, and
new things I now declare; before they
spring forth I tell you of them."
Isaiah 42:8-9 (ESV)

Christ came to love us so well so we
could love *ourselves* and *others* well.

"Blessed is she who *believed,* that
there would be a fulfillment of what
was spoken to her from the Lord."
Luke 1:45 (ESV)

chapter eight

When we have nothing to hide, we create *intimacy*.

Our trials push us to become the *greatest* version of ourselves.

"And let us not grow weary of doing *good*, for in due season we will *reap*, if we do not give up."
Galatians 6:9 (ESV)

We don't take territory back when we try to fight the enemy. We take territory back when we *believe*.

"They may be called oaks of righteousness, the planting of the Lord, that he may be *glorified.* They shall build up the ancient ruins; they shall raise up the former devastations; they shall repair the ruined cities, the devastations of many generations."
Isaiah 61:3b-4 (ESV)

Acknowledgments

When I was writing, *The Beautiful Ugly Truth*, I thought I was just journaling my thoughts and prayers. But God saw years down the road, beyond all of our pain and said, "I can use this to help others." Shame likes to hide in the corner of your heart and whisper to you that you are all alone. Not many people would allow someone else to tell part of their story. Mark Brague... you are the strongest man I know.

Since founding Reconnecting Lives Ministries, we discovered many others who suffer in silence. Our hearts are to come alongside other couples who feel betrayed by circumstances of life and point them to hope.

Jesus. Without you, this story would have been so different. I learned unconditional love through your Word.

Elijah and Kasey. I love you and for you both, I fought. I knew one day God would bring someone special into your life, son. We love Kasey like she has always been a part of us. Dad and I always want to be a real life example of "Brague's don't quit." I will love you both for the rest of my life.

Noah. I love you, son. For you I fought. I love watching God move in your life and how you allow Him to. Remember you will never lose in life. You will either win or you will learn. I promise, I will love you the rest of my life. **Reed.** Thank you for being a very special person in our family lives. You bring so much life.

Carol and Dean. Thank you for your constant friendship and support. Especially during the most difficult season of our marriage. You came to our rescue and stopped us from free falling that fateful night. Our lives are richer and brighter because of your friendship.

Dr. Sandy. The best licensed mental health counselor whom God picked out just for us. I know many lives have been changed because of your calling. Mark and I will forever be grateful for how you counseled us, walked alongside us, and left a deposit in us we will never be able to repay. Your wisdom and support were life changing.

Linda Charlene. You're my sister. Thank you for loving me enough and not letting me crash and burn.

Jennifer W. Thank you for seeing this book and its potential in me before anyone else. I will never forget the many breakfasts, phone calls, and sitting in the sun room of our rented house to get the outline started. Also, thanks to your sweet mom, Sharon, who gave up a quiet weekend at her house so the messy birthing of this book could begin.

Ginger and Tim. You walked with us through some very dark, murky days. Thank you for the days you let me "get it out." It was not always pretty but you both stayed close to our sides. I love how you find beauty and speak to it daily. Never stop being you. You are my favorite free-spirit.

Donita and Marc. You show up in my life at pivotal times and it is usually to pray me through. Thank you for your friendship and your unwavering faith in a good God.

Jen and David D. Thank you for your purity of heart to Jesus and your friends. You came into our lives and became the best roadies calling us to the finish line of this project with all your encouragement. Thank you for celebrating every milestone

Tuesday night Bible Study Ladies. Thank you for hearing about God's dream for me to be a published author and completely agreed that all things are possible. It seemed so far off, and yet, you believed with me.

Peggy M and Pam F. Thank you for reading the very first manuscript in the rawest form and helping me make sense out of it. You ladies were my very first editors.

Riverstone Church Staff and Body. Many of you will never know how you walked with us through some of our darkest days. You are a shining light for everyone who walks through your doors. Tom and Melissa T, Terry and Patty C, and the Thursday morning prayer ladies, I will forever be grateful for loving us and seeing past our pain. Jesus did the miraculous through you.

Restoration Church family, Pastor Chuck and Candance. Thank you for your friendship but also for believing in us. God was not finished with us. You are consistent.

16:22 Men's Group. Thank you for hanging out and being accountable to one another. Men need a safe place to come in from the battle and take their armor off for a minute. You guys rock. I am so thankful for each of you and the strength you create when you are all together.

Stephanie B and Reclaimed Ministries. Continue to tell your story. Porn kills intimacy. We are an army when we band together. I believe in you and so thankful for our meeting years ago at She Speaks.

Jodi R and Depth Podcast. Thank you for letting us tell our story first on your podcast.

Restored2More. Clinton and Charity. You guys are brave and courageous. Thank you for the interview but most importantly standing with us as we get the word out. Porn is not healthy and destroys marriages. God's blessings and protection as you go. (Joshua 1:9)

Marriage Today. So grateful. Thank you for every hurdle you have crossed. Your ministry is so valuable. We were a shell of a couple when we found you on TV. And your ministry nursed us back to health. We are honored to be 'Marriage on the Rock' coaches helping other hurting couples.

Revolution Church. Our lives are richer because of you!!!

Anna R. Thank you for your talents and gifting to the world. And thank you for the cover.

Two Penny Publishing and Team. Tom G, Jodi C, Sarah W and Kaylee S.

Thank you for believing in me and our story. I am amazed, the more we talk about it, the more people tell us about their secret journey. "The light shines in the darkness, and the darkness has not overcome it." (John 1:5 NIV) Thank you for your "Yes" to publishing...many other yeses are following.

About Reconnecting Lives Ministries

Gwen Brague is co-founder of Reconnecting Lives Ministries with her husband and pastor, Mark Brague. Their home and ministry is located in Atlanta Georgia. RLM exists to be a friend of couples and marriages new and old. Whether you are just getting starting in marriage or have years of experience, our team will walk by your side to encourage you along your journey back to health in your marriage through:

- marriage coaching
- books and resources
- bible studies
- zoom chats
- daily devotions

For more information about
Reconnecting Lives Ministries, visit
www.reconnectinglives.org

About the Author

Gwen Brague is a wife, a mom, a friend, bestselling author and co-founder of Reconnecting Lives Ministries. She loves Jesus, her husband, her two man-cubs and all kinds of God's people. She believes nothing is too hard to accomplish if you put your mind to it and is passionate about seeing hurting marriages reconnect and recapture their first love.